Easy KEYTAB Method

I0799941

KIDS SONGS

Written & Method By:
John McCarthy

Envision with us.
ARTSWESTCT

Supervising Editor: John McCarthy
Music Arrangements: Damiano Christian & John McCarthy
Music Transcribing & Engraving: Damiano Christian
Production Manager: John McCarthy
Layout, Graphics, & Design: Jimmy Rutkowski
Copy Editors:
Cathy McCarthy & John McCarthy

Cover Art Direction & Design:
Jimmy Rutkowski

ISBN: 979-8-218-48990-8
Produced by McCarthy Publishing

Table of Contents

About the Author

John Frederick McCarthy is a musician, author, educator and creator of the Rock House Method system of learning. Since 2001, The Rock House Method has sold more than three million instructional programs of which McCarthy writes, composes, and demonstrates in. McCarthy has developed a curriculum for learning to play music that covers guitar, piano, ukulele, drums, bass guitar, singing, children's early music development and music theory. Currently he has authored over 60 instructional method books and 58 instructional DVDs. In addition to his own instructional books and programs John has worked with many of the greatest musicians in the world creating personal instruction programs featuring the Rock House Method. John also is the founder/owner of the Rock House School of Music since 1981and is franchising and opening locations across America. In 2020 John McCarthy was awarded a patent for his revolutionary new way to read piano music called KEYTAB. The KEYTAB Piano system comes with a "KEYTAB Note Strip" and uses a unique color-coded sheet music to allow players to learn songs quickly and easily.

How to Use this Book

KEYTAB will help your child get started playing piano quickly and easily. Simply put the KEYTAB Note Strip behind the keys of any piano or electric keyboard and follow the color-coded music to start playing songs in minutes. Your child will learn how the piano is broken into octaves that repeat across the keyboard. This instantly helps children understand and memorize the note names and see how they follow a repetitive pattern. The KEYTAB Note Strip helps children transition to reading music. The notation for each note is included along with the note name on the note strip. You can also access video tutorials to help guide your child to play each song. Go to www.KeyTabMusic.com to get these video tutorials and many other popular songs.

How to Read KEYTAB

Get ready for the awesome world of KEYTAB – it's the magical key that makes playing cool songs and chords on the piano super easy! This modern music reading system is a shortcut to letting you groove to your favorite tunes in no time at all.

Now, here's the lowdown on KEYTAB: Imagine the staff on your sheet music is like a road, and right in the middle, there's a count bar telling you the beat of the song. The top part is for your right hand, and the bottom part is for your left hand. The letters tell you the note's name, and the colors show which part of the keyboard to play. Grab your KEYTAB Note Strip, slap it behind your piano keys, and match the colors – easy, right? Oh, and those numbers after each note? They're like your musical GPS, guiding your fingers where to go. It's as simple as that! Now go on, have a blast playing your favorite songs!

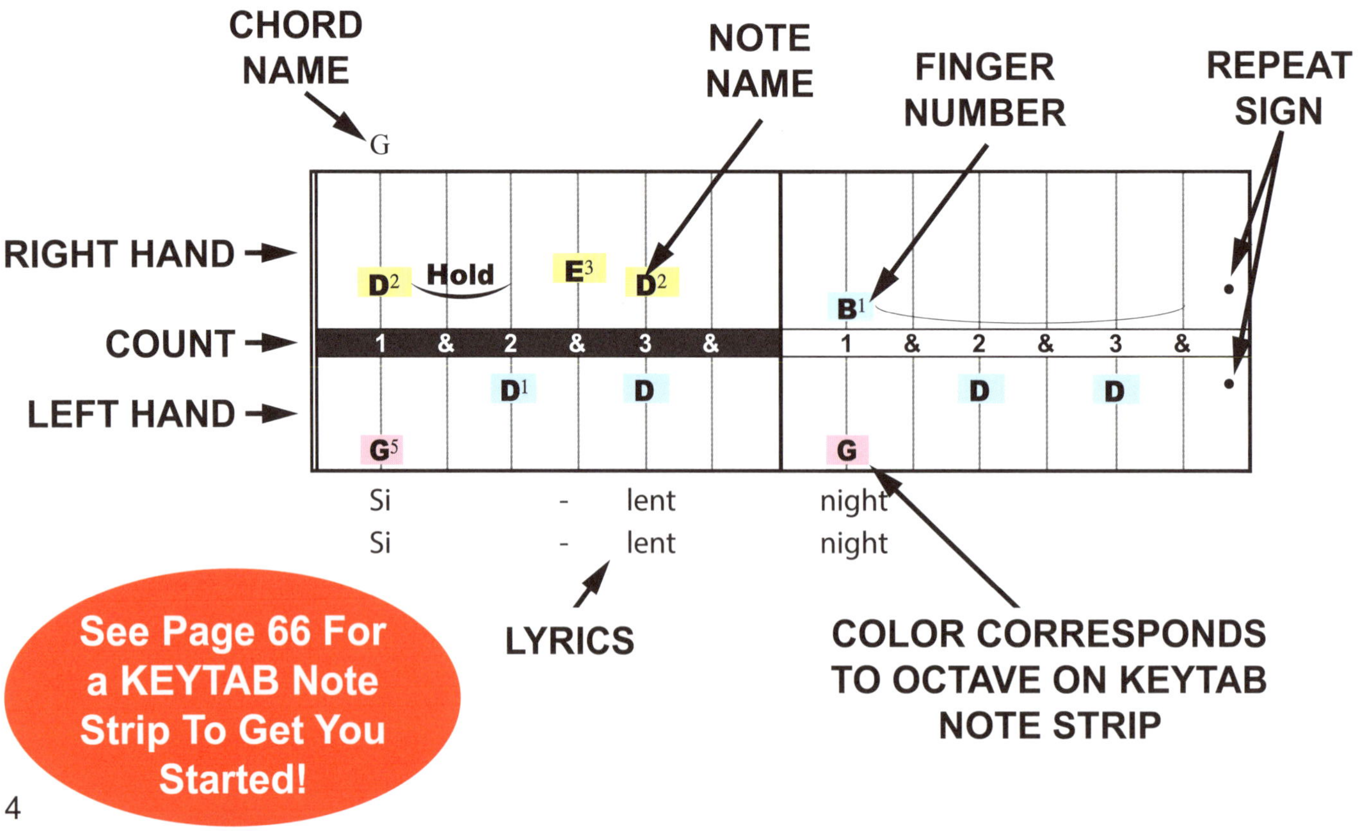

See Page 66 For a KEYTAB Note Strip To Get You Started!

Repeat Signs, Let Ring Slurs and Finger Numbers

In the songs featured in this book, you will encounter two common notations: repeat signs and hold slurs. A repeat sign directs you to go back and replay the same section before progressing beyond the sign to the next part of the music. If a section needs to be repeated multiple times, you will find a number above the final repeat sign indicating how many repetitions are required (see page 20). If no number is specified, repeat the section once and then proceed to the following part.

Hold slurs are used to signify that the key(s) being played should be sustained, allowing the notes to ring for the specified duration indicated by the count. For instance, in the first song of this book, "Hot Cross Buns," the first note E is played on the 1 count and then sustained for the "& 2 &" count. The second note D is played on the 3 count and should be held for the "& 4 &" count. The third note, "C," is played on the 1 count of the second measure and should be held for the "& 2 & 3 & 4 &" counts.

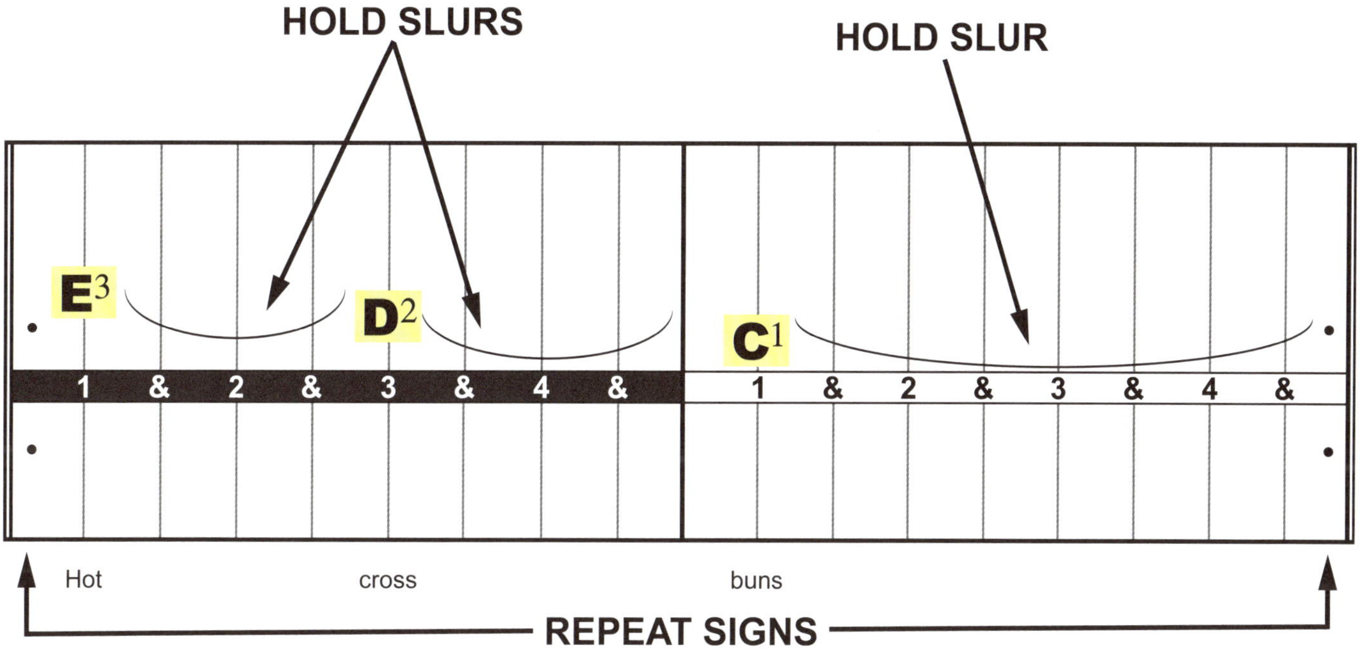

Finger Numbers

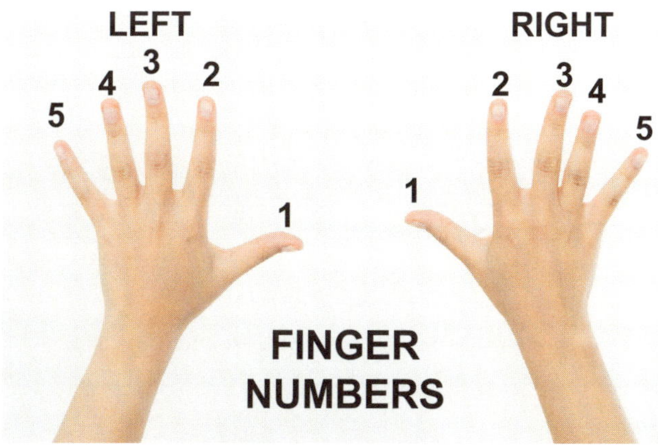

Access Your Video Lessons

Included with this book are video tutorials for each song. These tutorials go through each song slowly with close-up views and then each song is played at full speed. To access your video lessons go to **www.KeyTabMusic.com**.

Hot Cross Buns

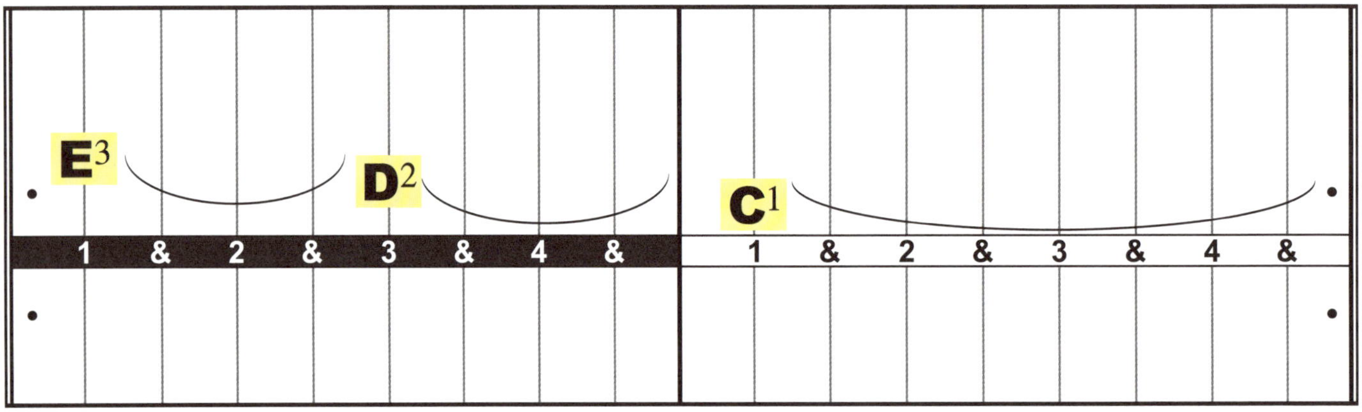

Hot cross buns

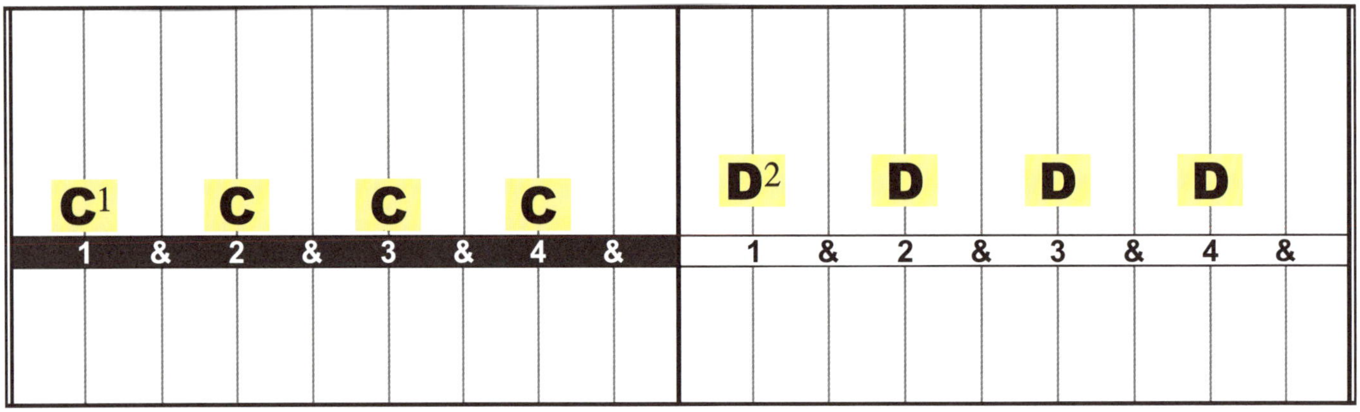

One a pen - ny, Two a pen - ny,

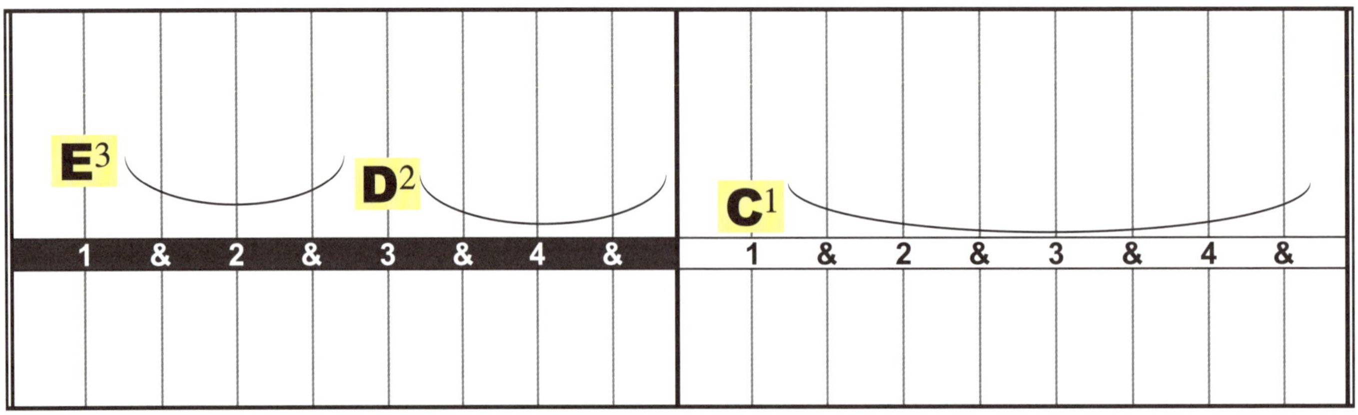

Hot cross buns

Rain, Rain Go Away

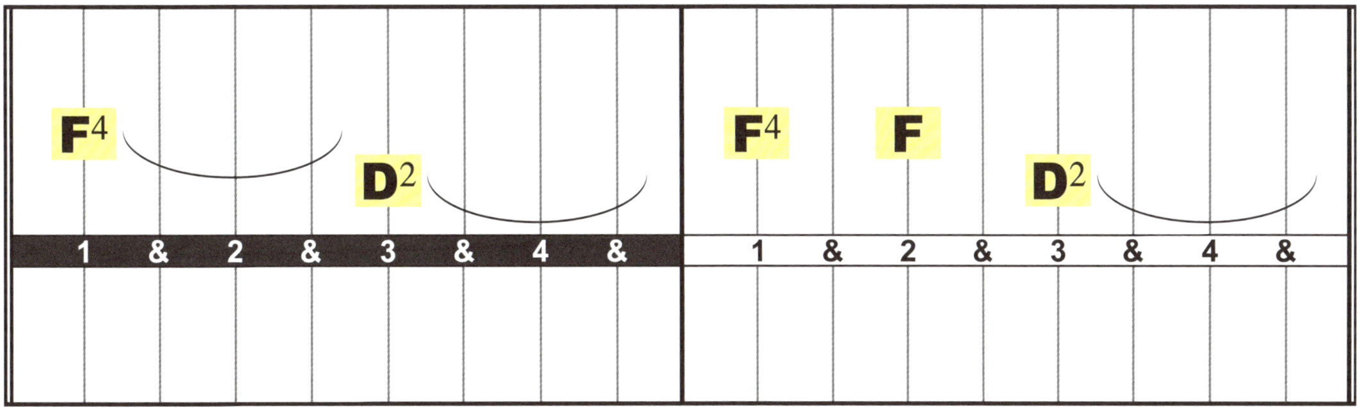

Rain, ________ Rain, ________ Go a — way ________

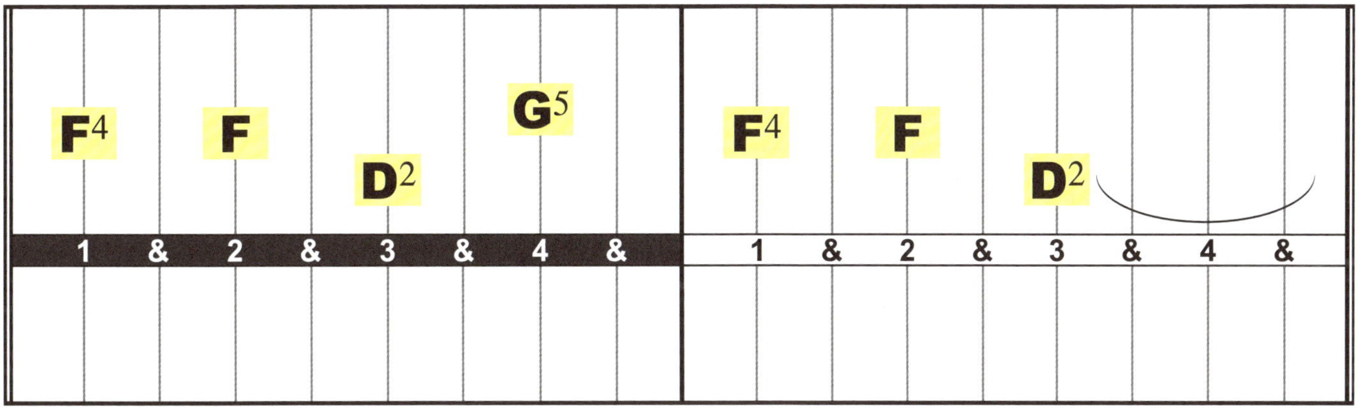

Come a — gain some o — ther day. ________

Mary Had a Little Lamb

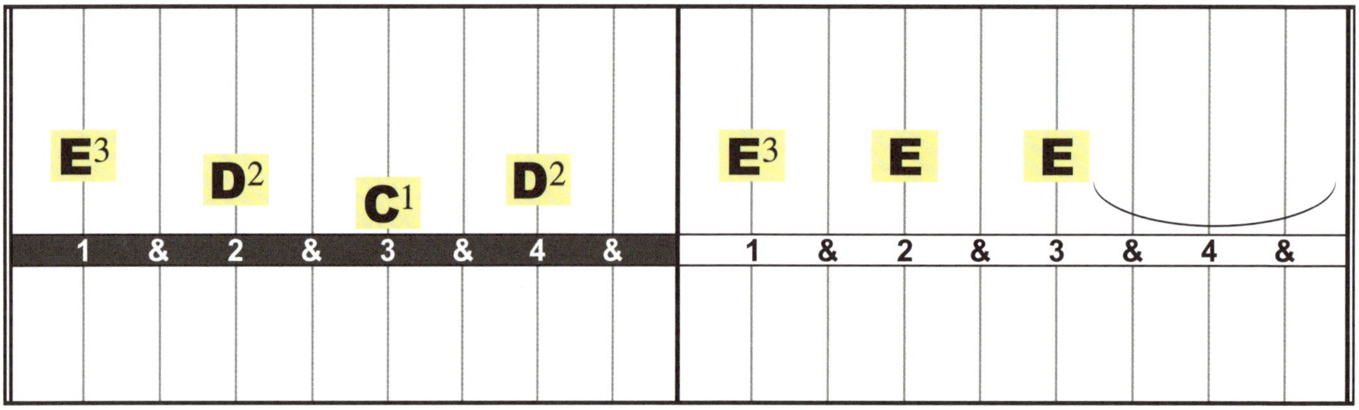

Ma - ry had a lit - tle lamb,

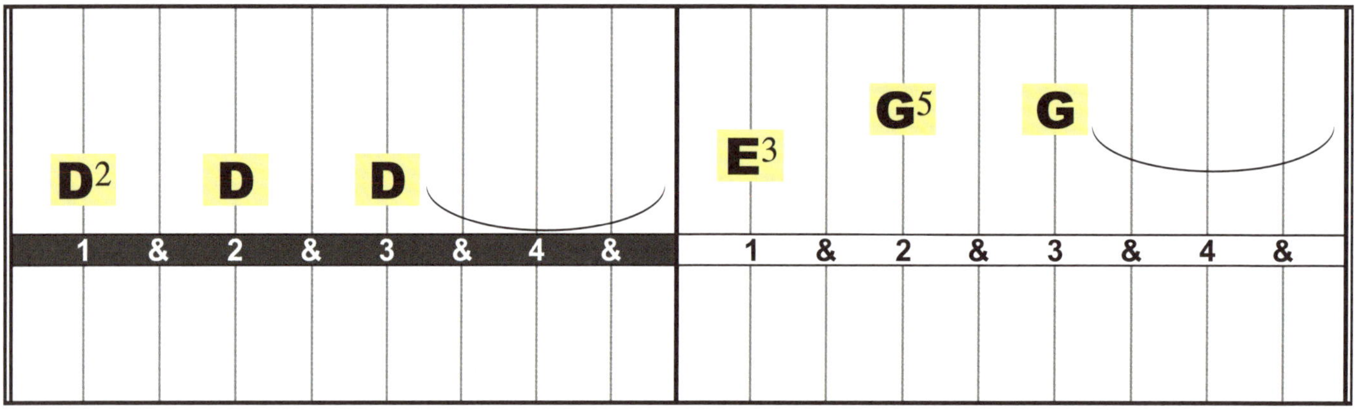

lit - tle lamb, lit - tle lamb.

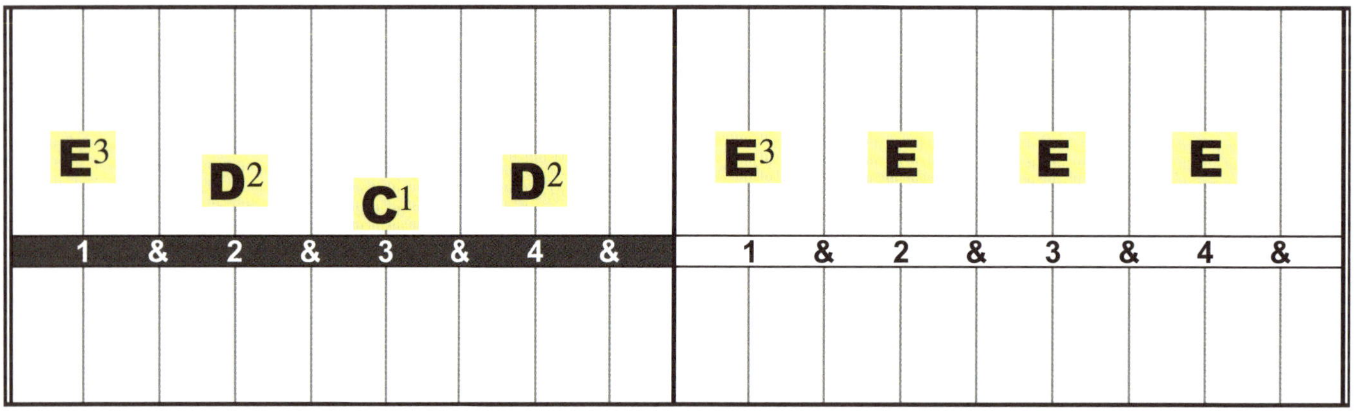

Ma - ry had a lit - tle lamb it's

D^2		D		E^3		D^2		C^1							
1	&	2	&	3	&	4	&	1	&	2	&	3	&	4	&
fleece		was		white		as		snow ______________________________.							

Jingle Bells

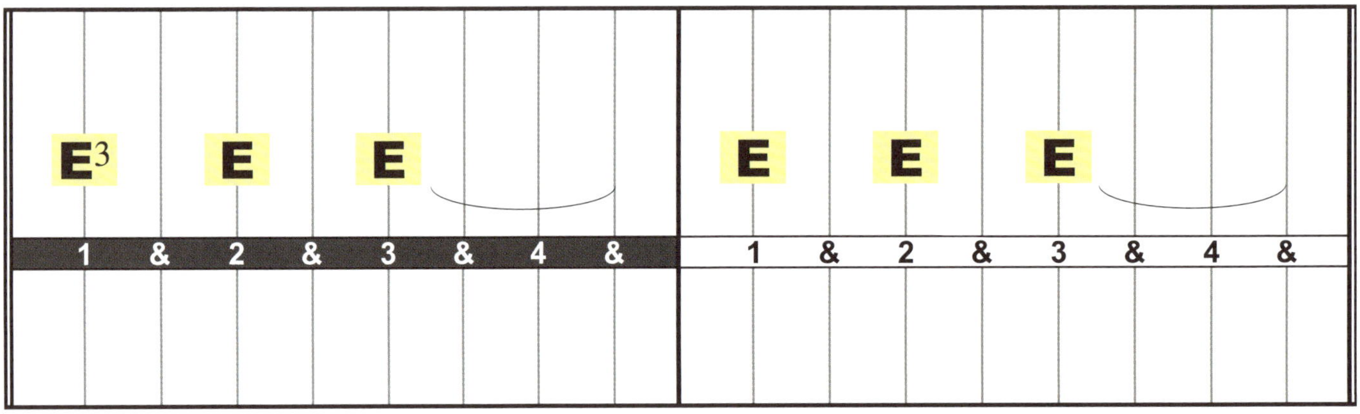

Jin - gle Bells Jin - gle Bells

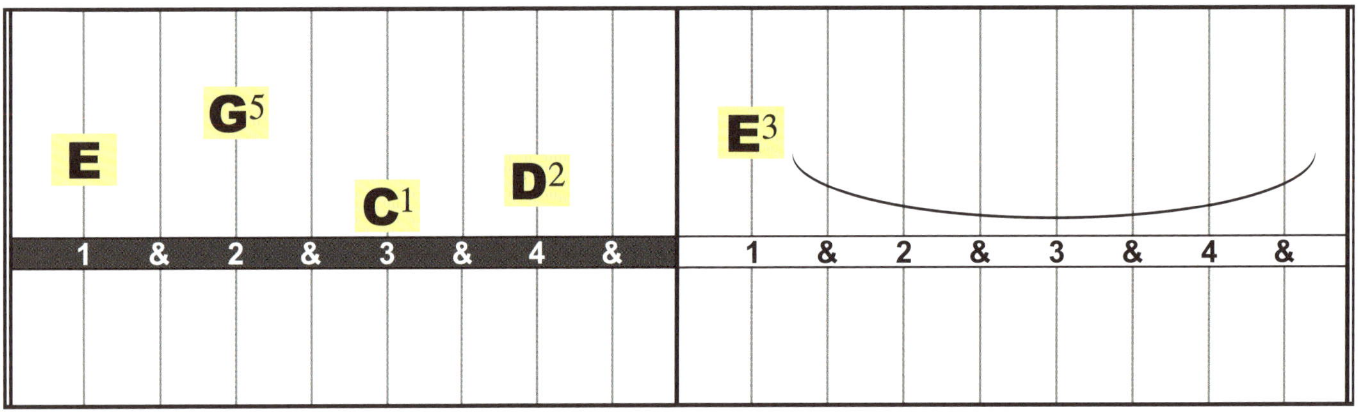

Jin - gle all the way ____________________________________ .

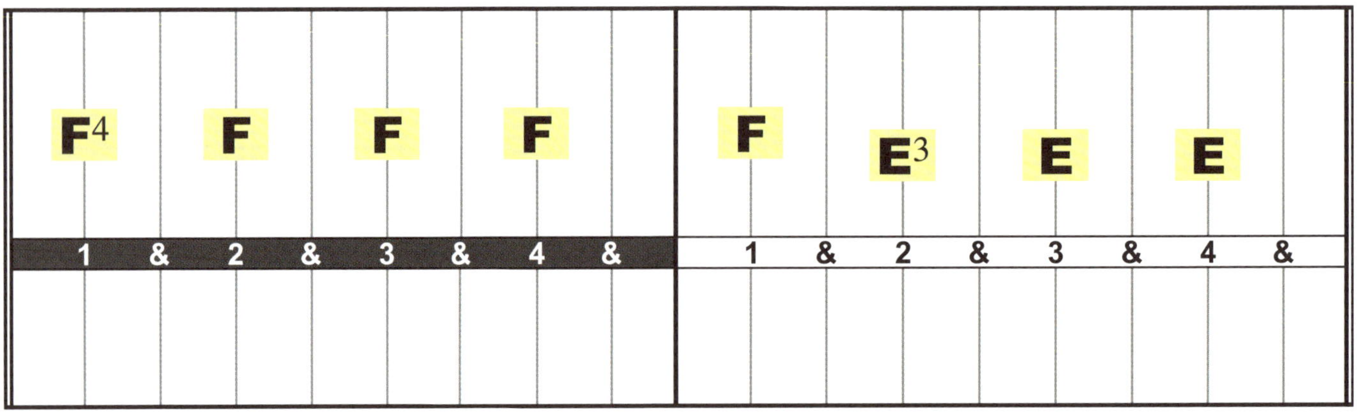

Oh what fun it is to ride in a

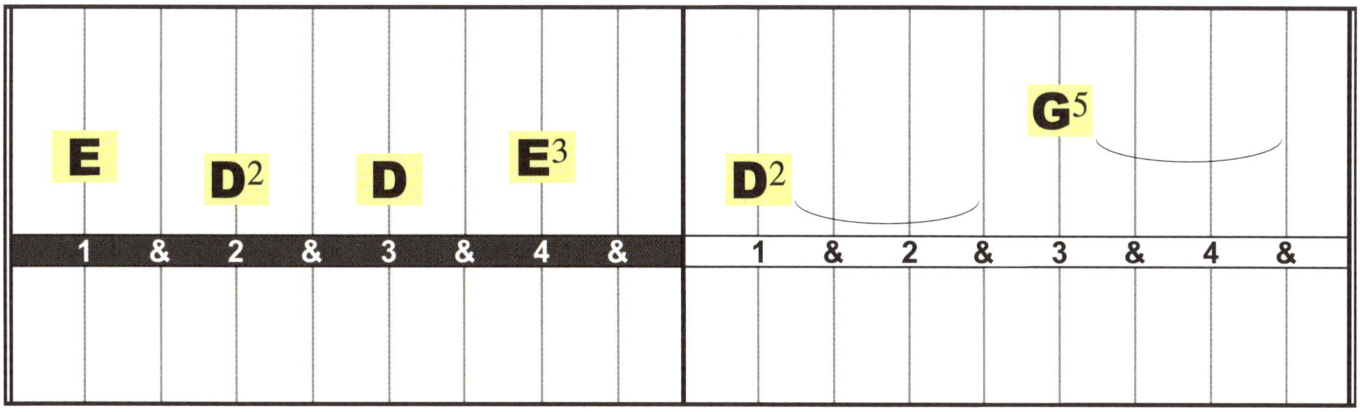

one horse o - pen sleigh hey!

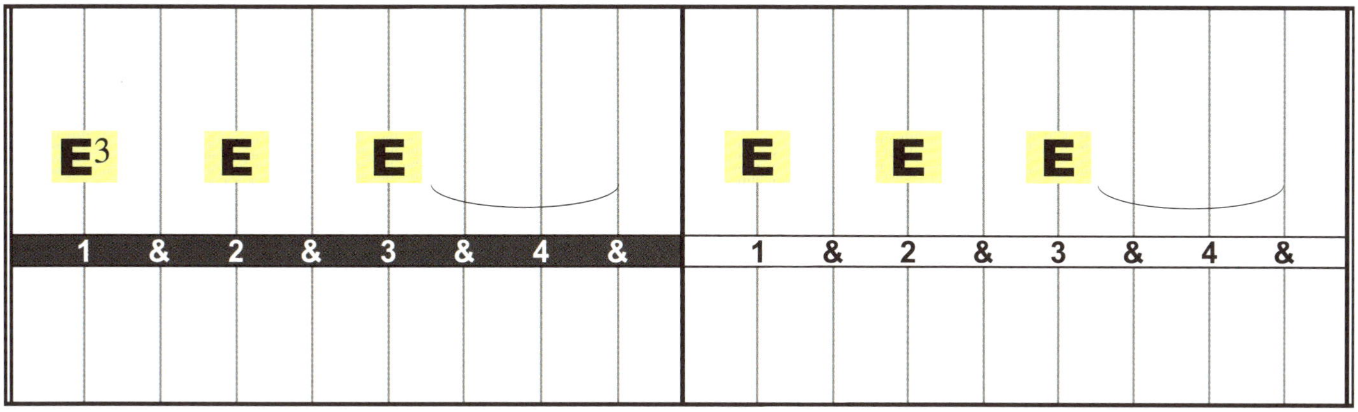

Jin - gle Bells Jin - gle Bells

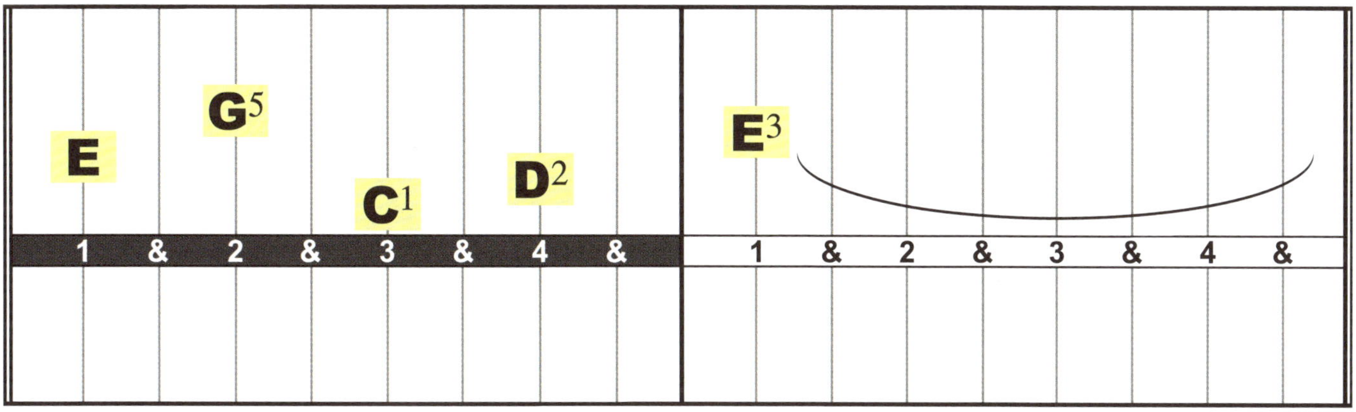

Jin - gle all the way ______________________________.

1	&	2	&	3	&	4	&	1	&	2	&	3	&	4	&
F[4]		F		F		F		F		E[3]		E		E	
Oh		what		fun		it		is		to		ride		in	a

1	&	2	&	3	&	4	&	1	&	2	&	3	&	4	&
G[5]		G		F[4]		D[2]		C[1]							
one		horse		o	-	pen		sleigh.							

A Tisket, A Tasket

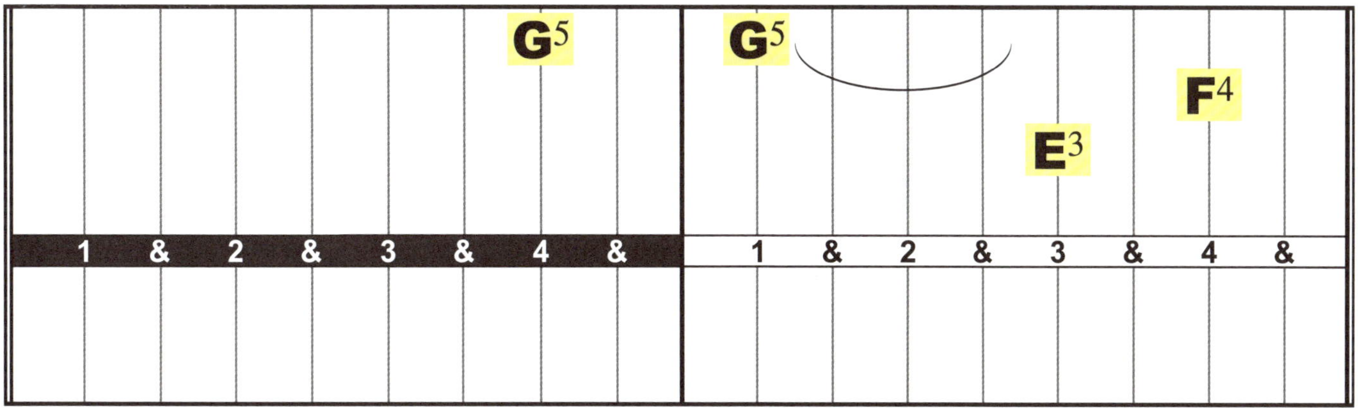

A Tis ——— ket. A

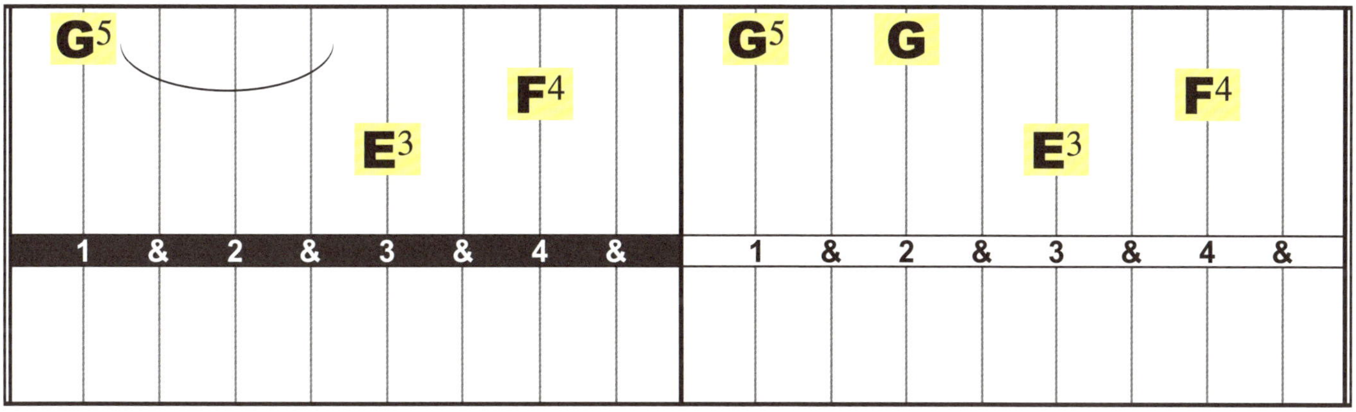

Tas ——— ket. A green and yell - ow

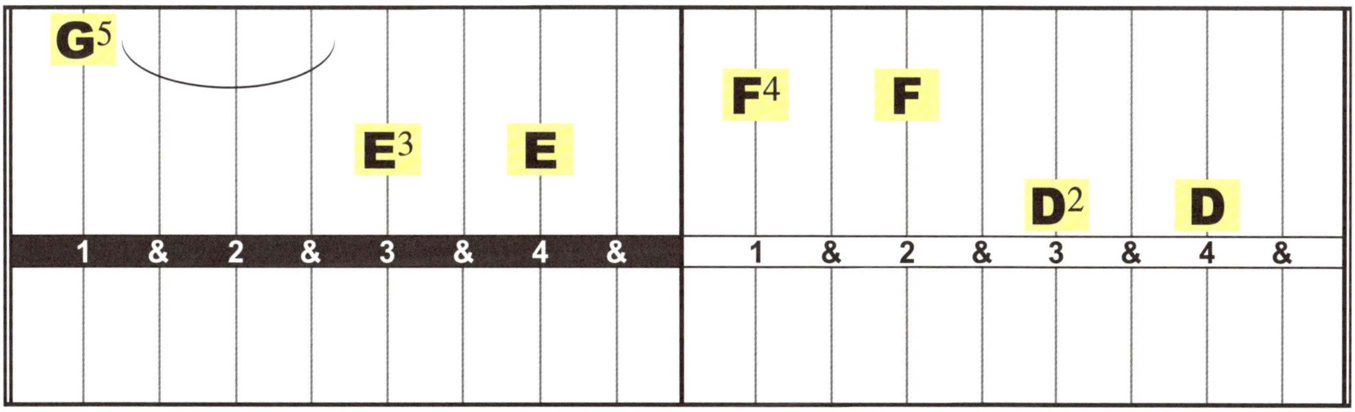

bas ——— ket, I wrote a let - ter

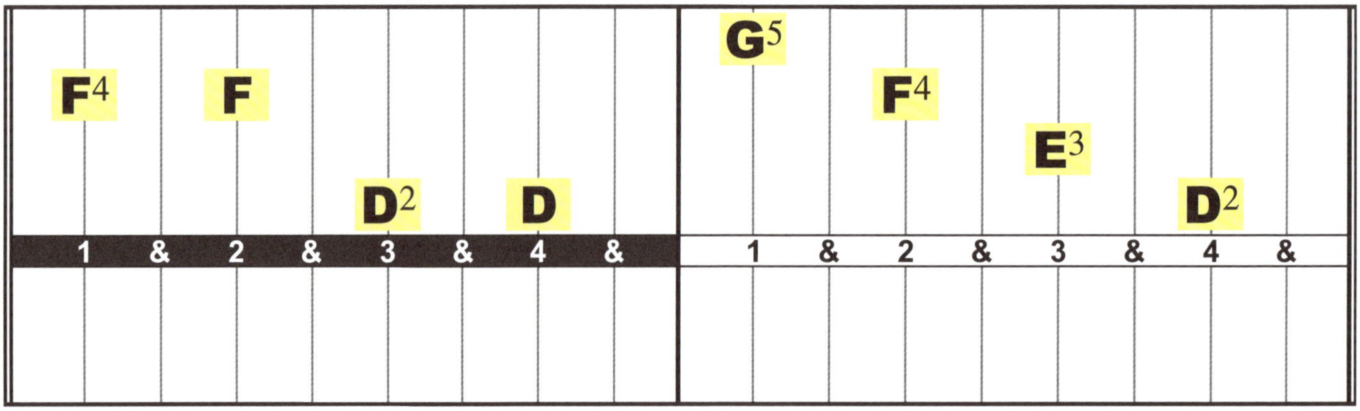

to my love, and on my way I

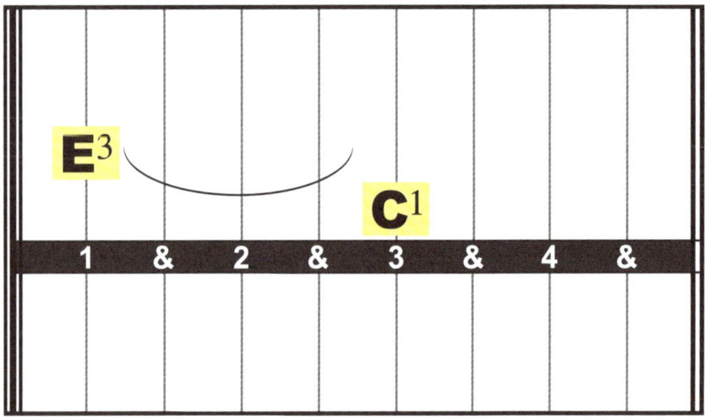

dropped ———— it.

Oh When the Saints

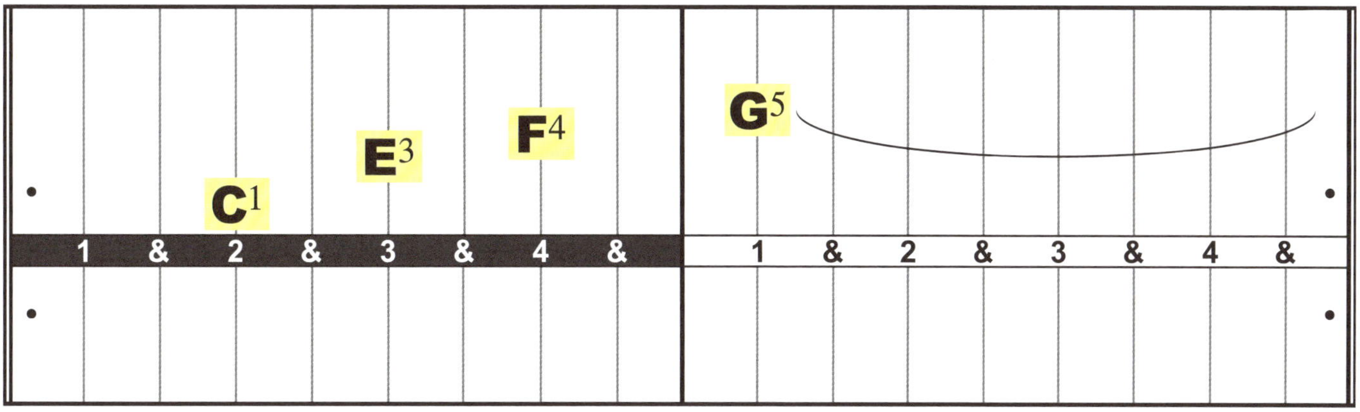

Oh, when the saints

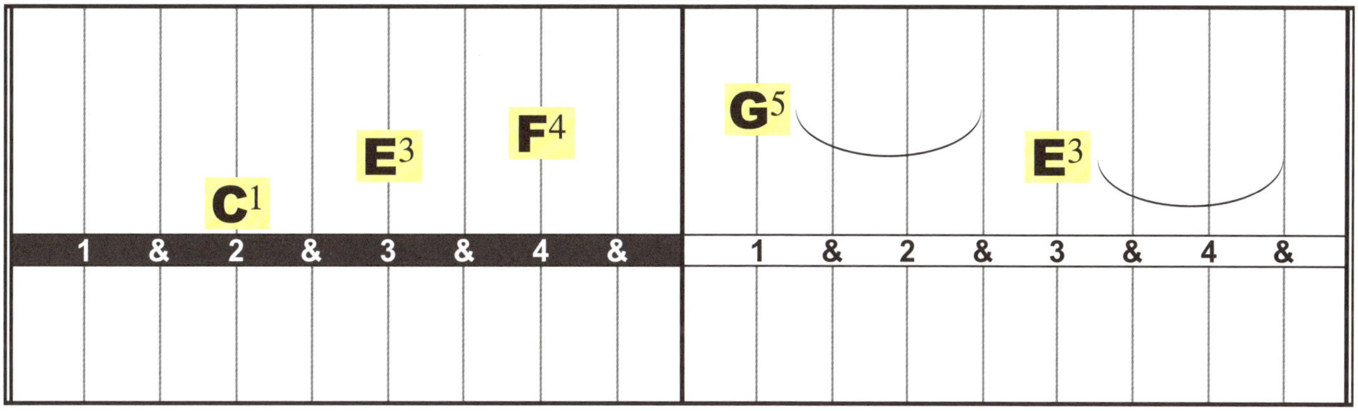

Oh, when the Saints go

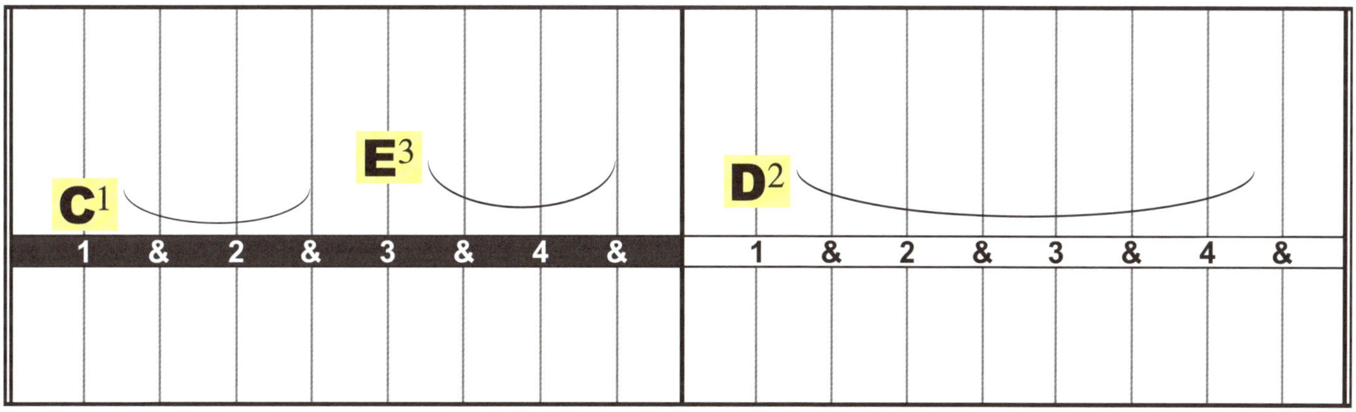

march — ing ______ in ______

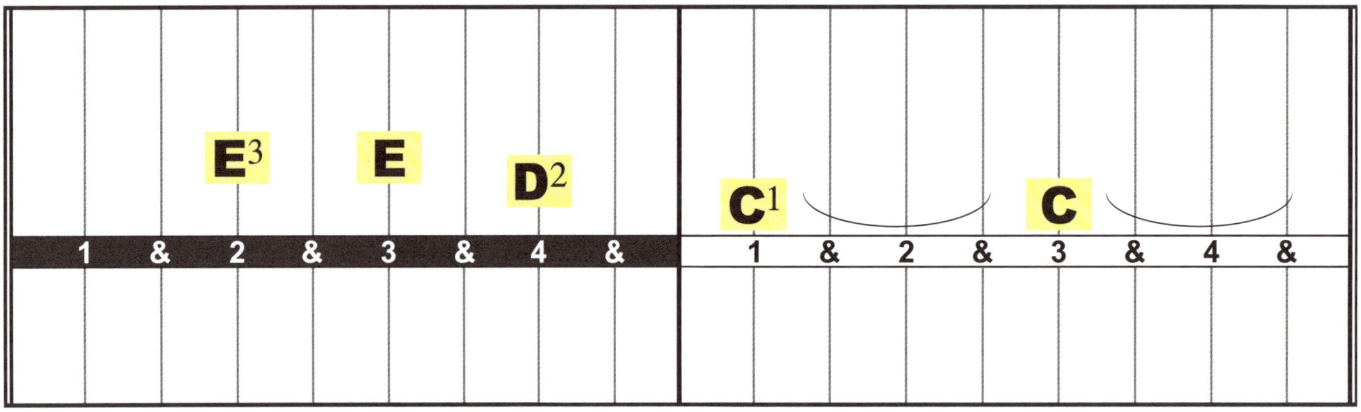

Oh, Lord I want ______ to ______

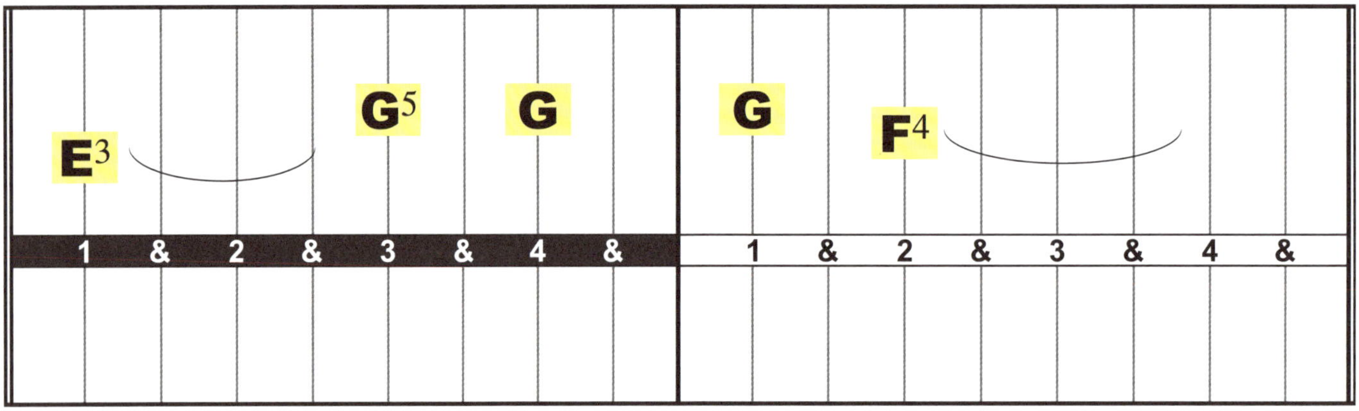

be ______ in that num — ber ______

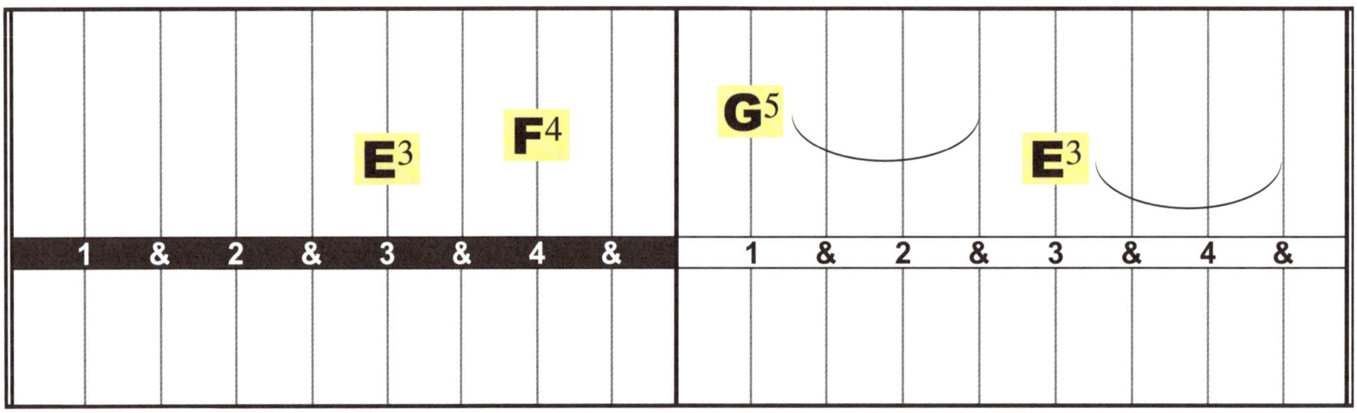

When the Saints ______ go ______

D^2				D				C^1							
1	&	2	&	3	&	4	&	1	&	2	&	3	&	4	&

march — ing ______ in ______.

Miss Mary Mack

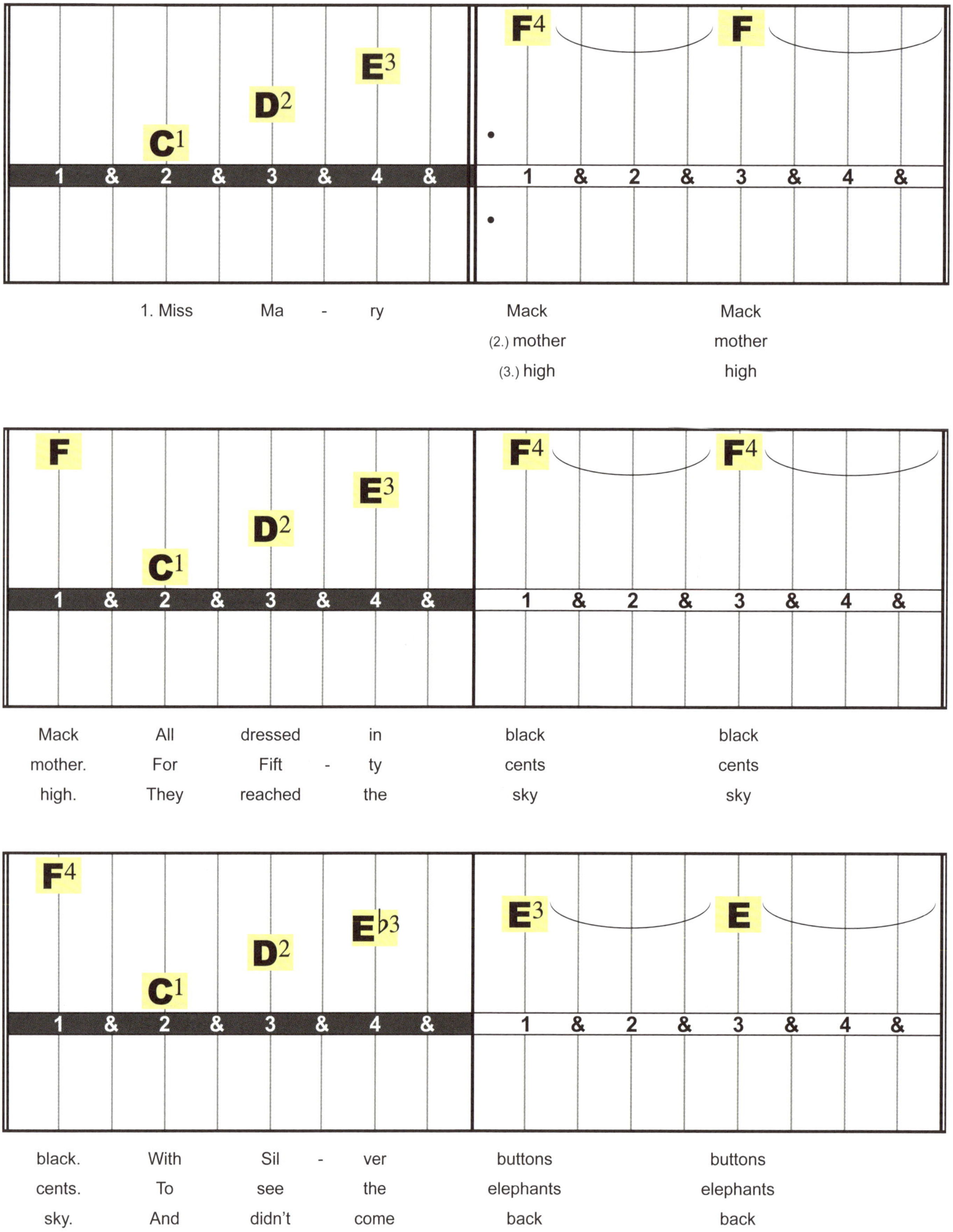

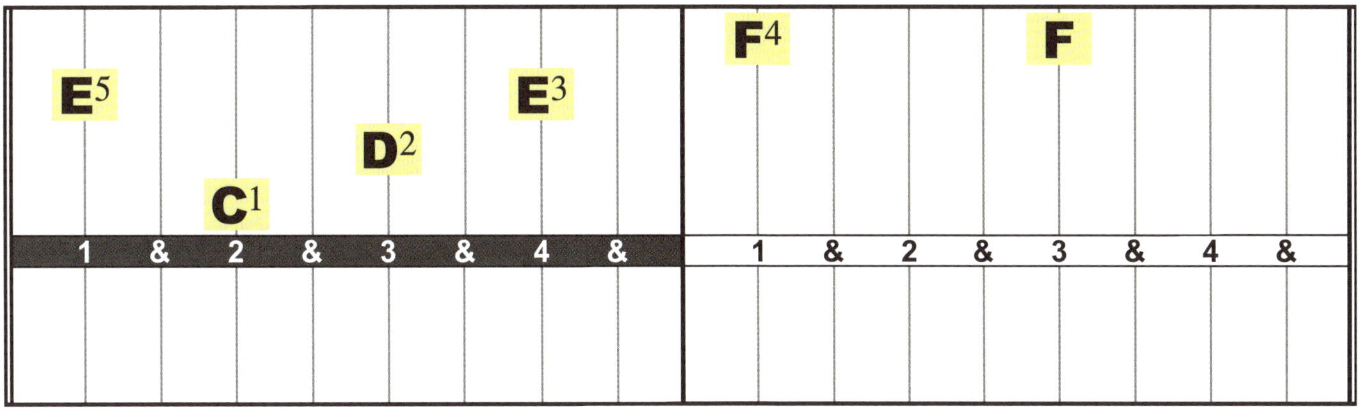

buttons. All down her back back
elephants. Jump over the fence fence
black. Til' the Fourth-of Ju - ly - ly

Repeat 3x

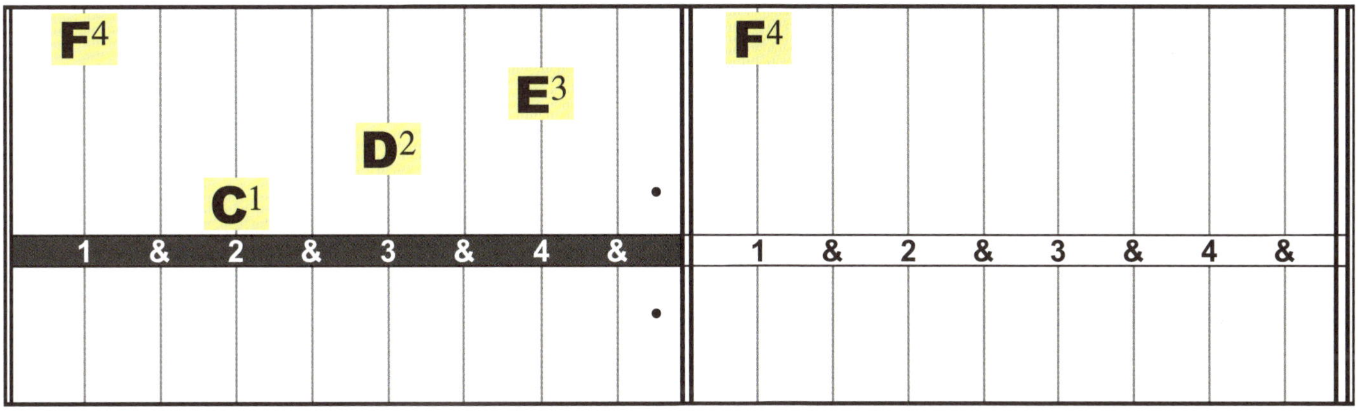

back.
fence 2. She asked her
3. They jumped so - ly.

The Alphabet Song

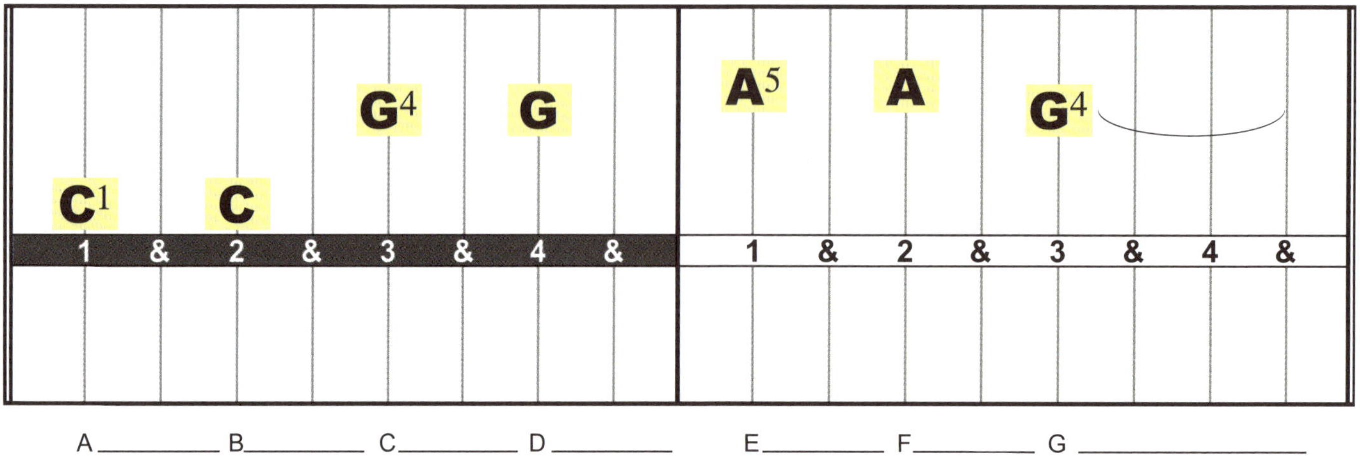

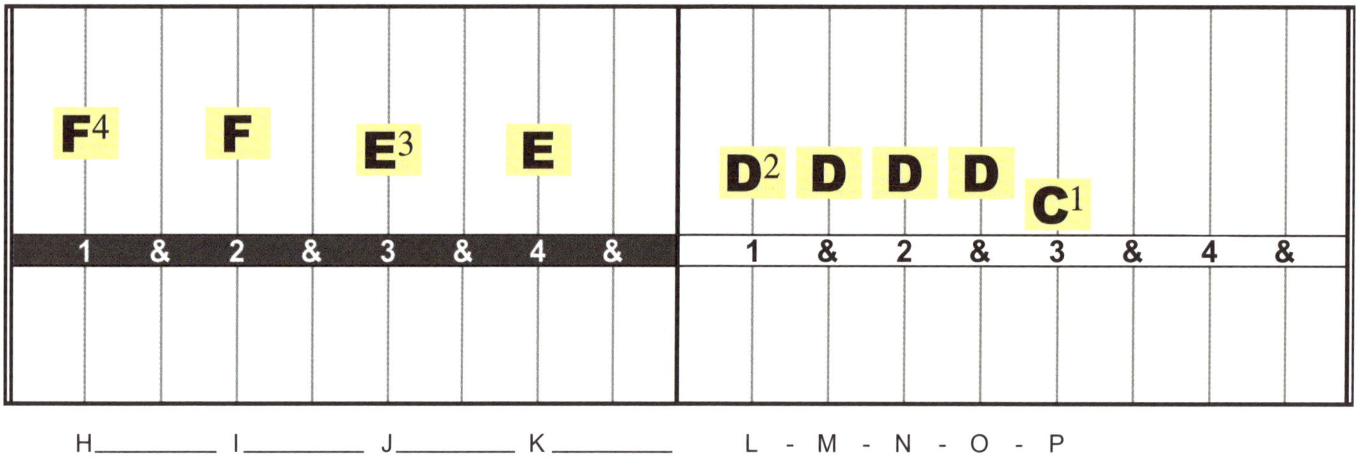

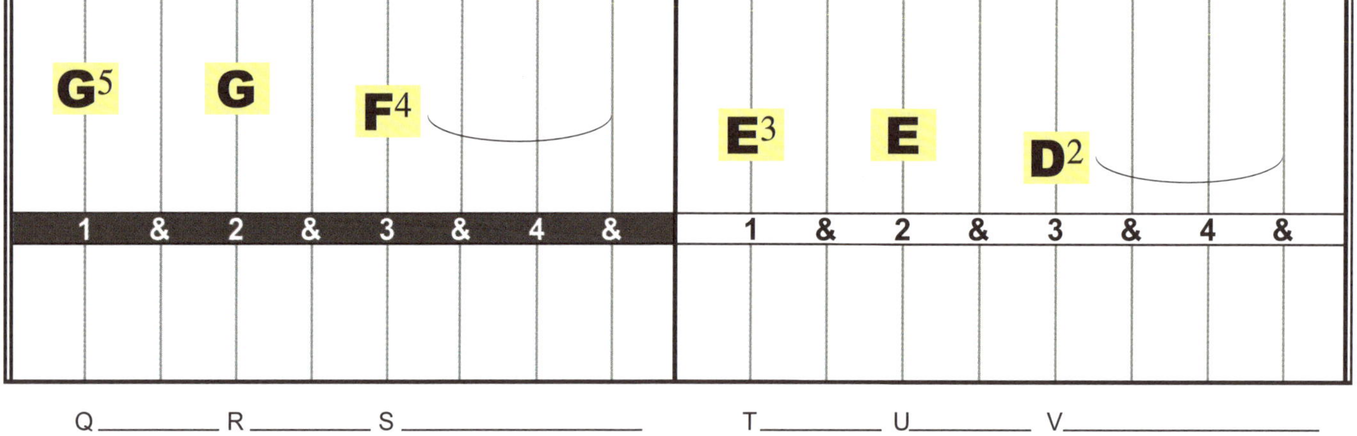

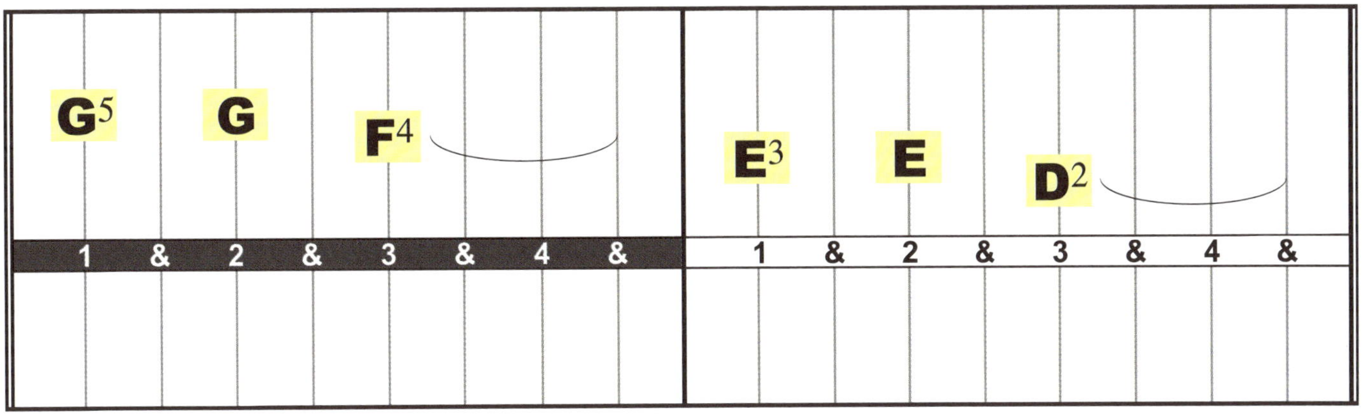

W________________ X Y________ and____ Z________

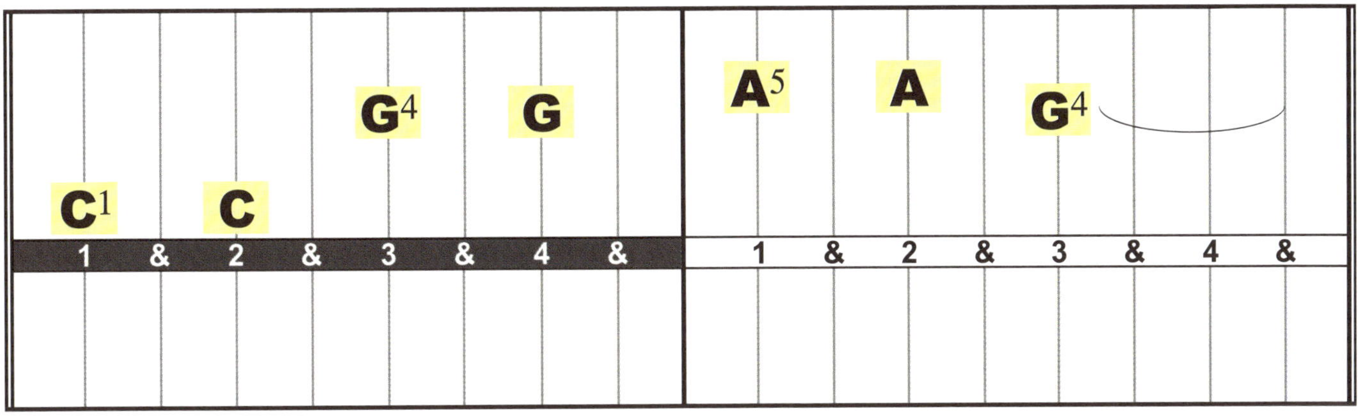

Now I know my A - B - C's

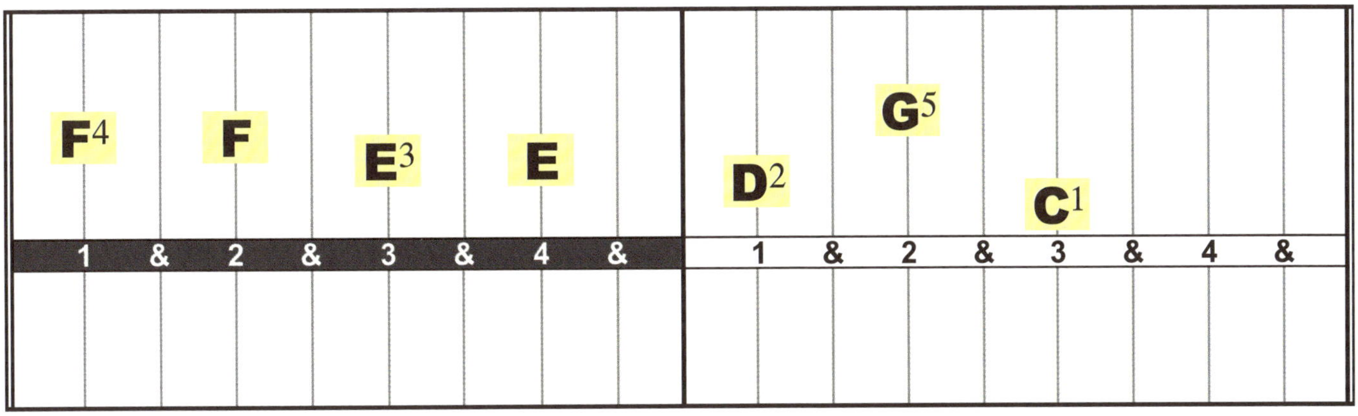

Next time won't you sing with me?

This Old Man

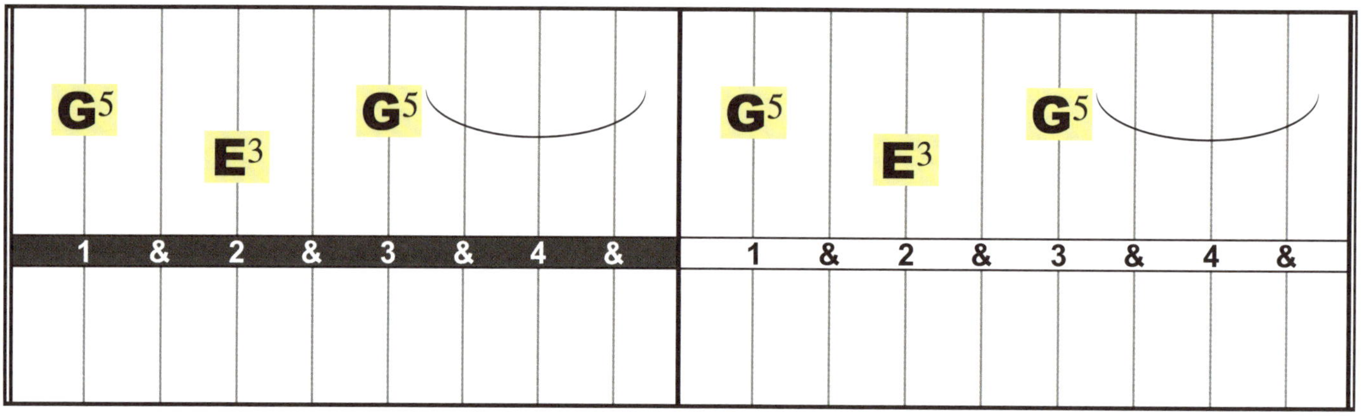

This old man, he played one,

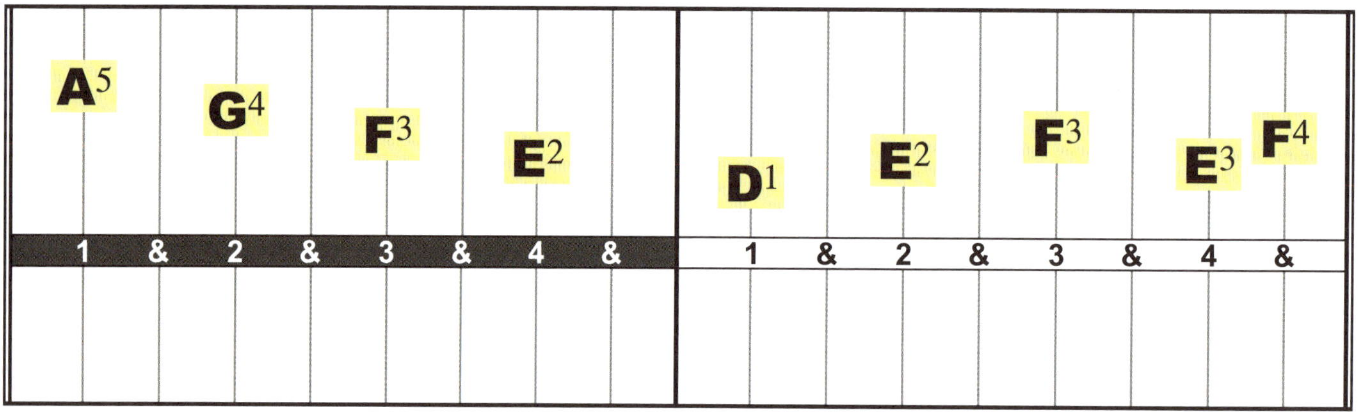

He played knick - knack on my thumb; with a

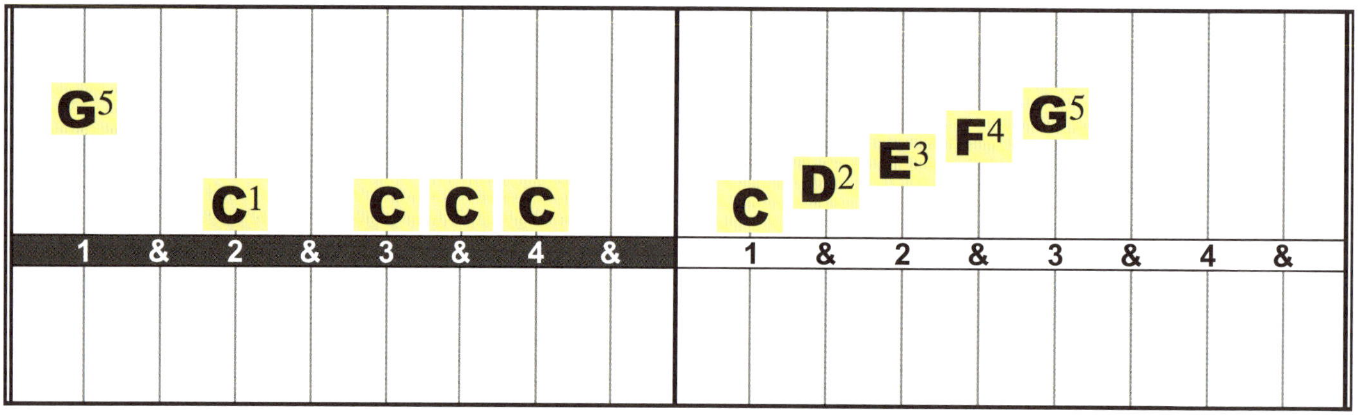

knick - knack pad - dy whack, give the dog a bone,

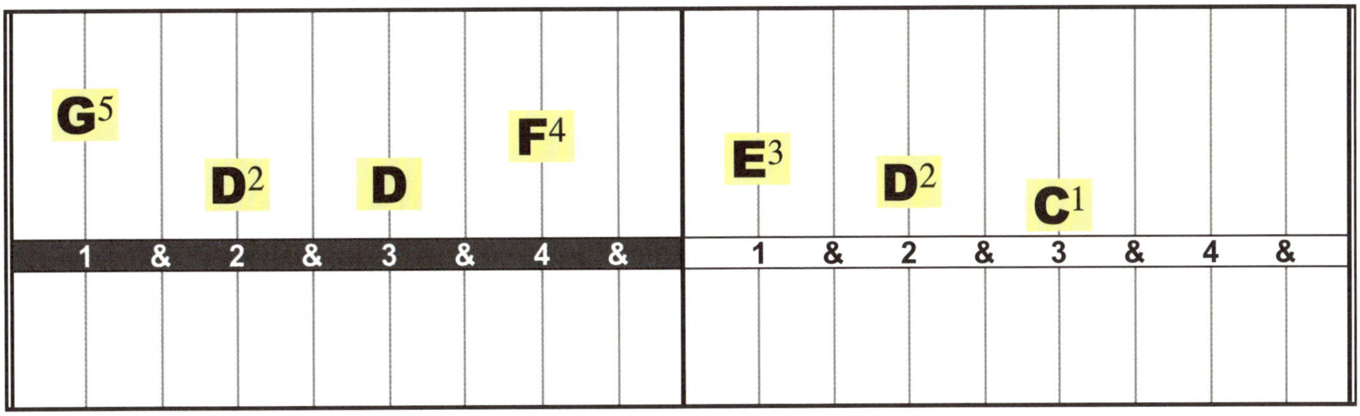

This old man came roll - ing home.

Verse 2
This old man, he played two,
He played knick-knack on my shoe;
With a knick-knack paddywhack,
Give the dog a bone,
This old man came rolling home.

Verse 3
This old man, he played three,
He played knick-knack on my knee;
With a knick-knack paddywhack,
Give the dog a bone,
This old man came rolling home.

Verse 4
This old man, he played four,
He played knick-knack on my door;
With a knick-knack paddywhack,
Give the dog a bone,
This old man came rolling home.

Verse 5
This old man, he played five,
He played knick-knack on my hive;
With a knick-knack paddywhack,
Give the dog a bone,
This old man came rolling home.

Verse 6
This old man, he played six,
He played knick-knack on my sticks;
With a knick-knack paddywhack,
Give the dog a bone,
This old man came rolling home.

Verse 7
This old man, he played seven,
He played knick-knack up in heaven;
With a knick-knack paddywhack,
Give the dog a bone,
This old man came rolling home..

Verse 8
This old man, he played eight,
He played knick-knack on my gate;
With a knick-knack paddywhack,
Give the dog a bone,
This old man came rolling home.

Verse 9
This old man, he played nine,
He played knick-knack on my spine;
With a knick-knack paddywhack,
Give the dog a bone,
This old man came rolling home.

Verse 10
This old man, he played ten,
He played knick-knack once again;
With a knick-knack paddywhack,
Give the dog a bone,
This old man came rolling home.

You are My Sunshine

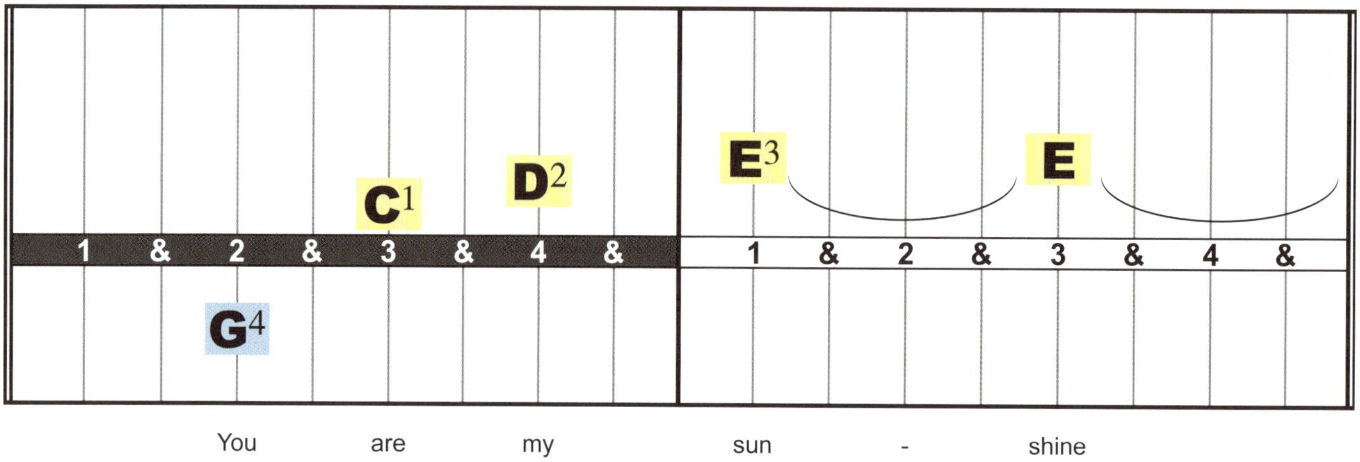

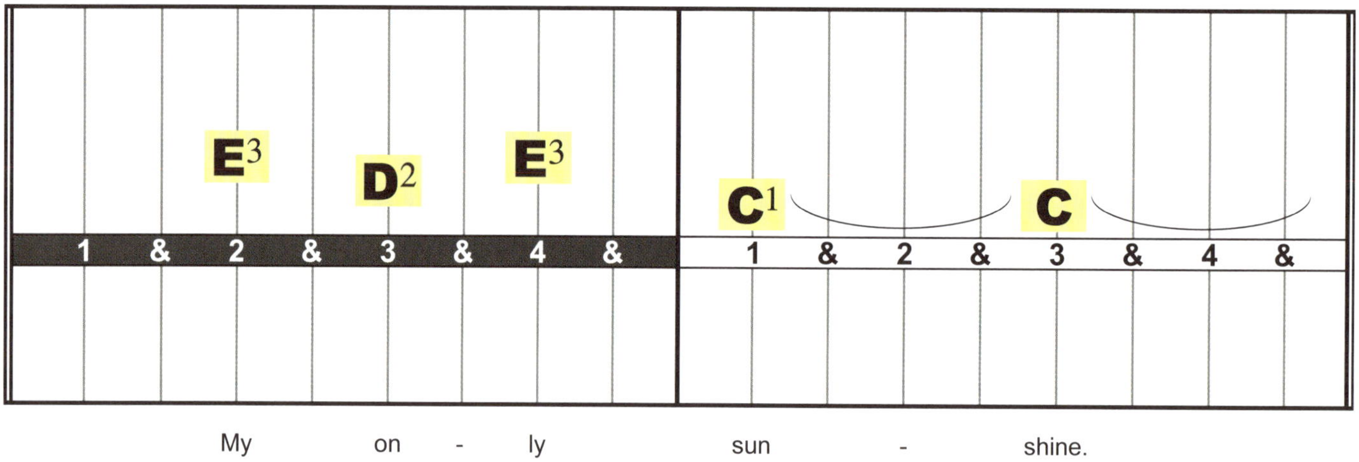

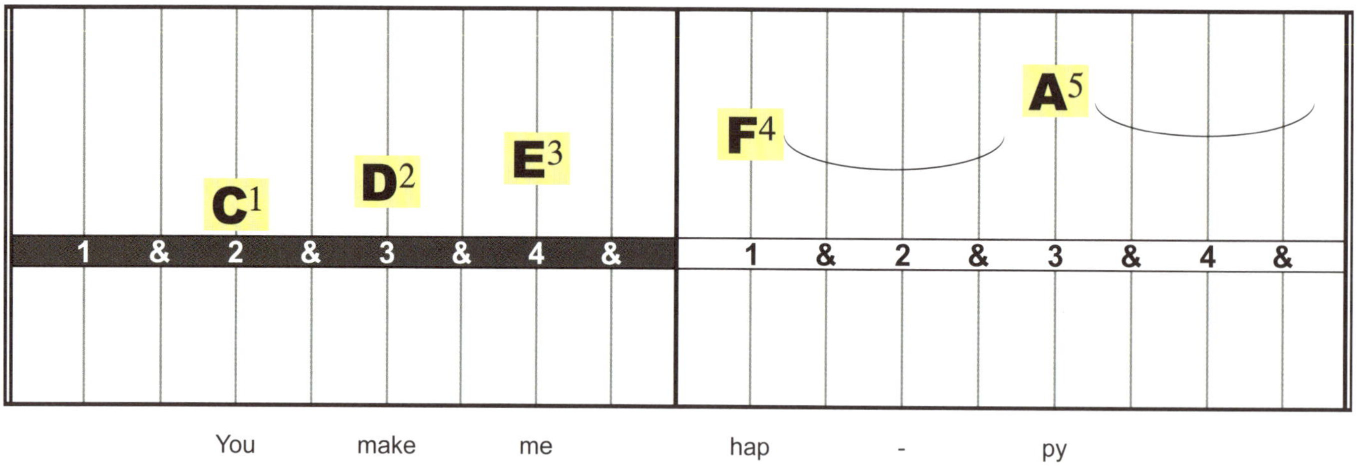

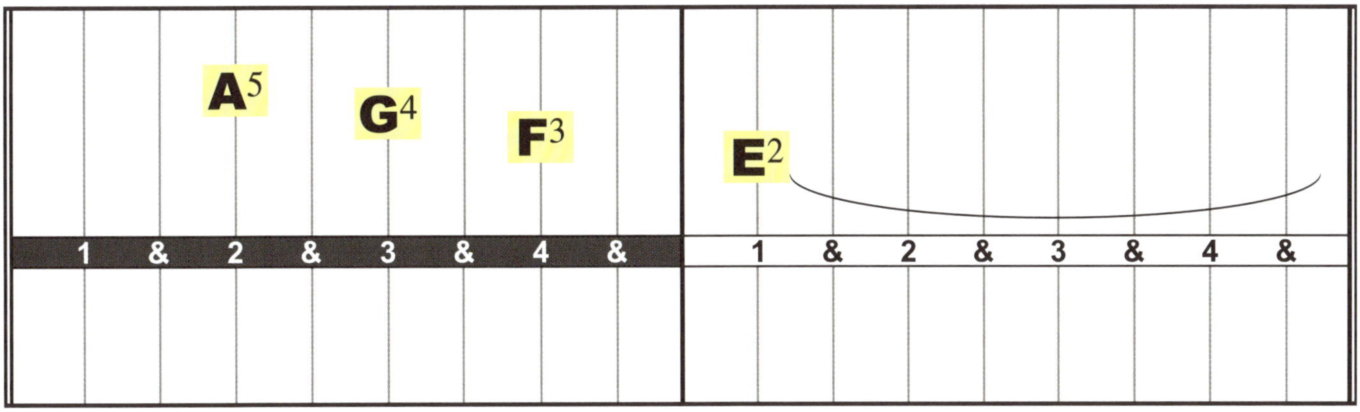

When skies are grey.

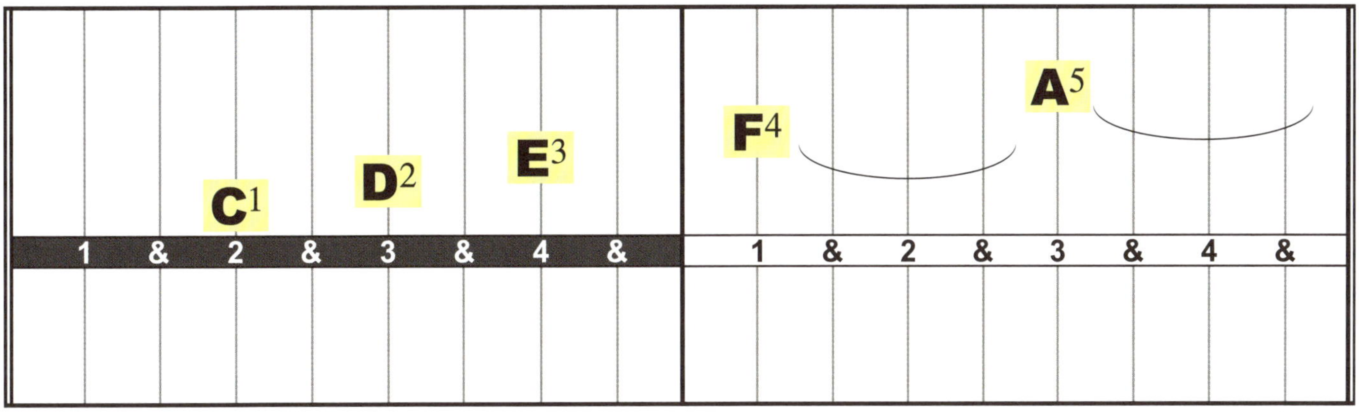

You ne - ver know dear

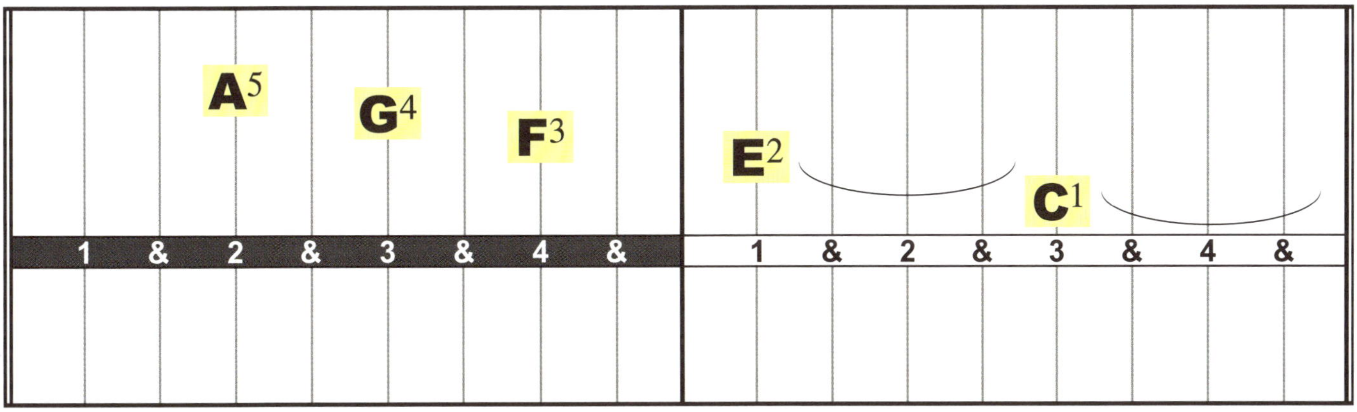

How much I love you.

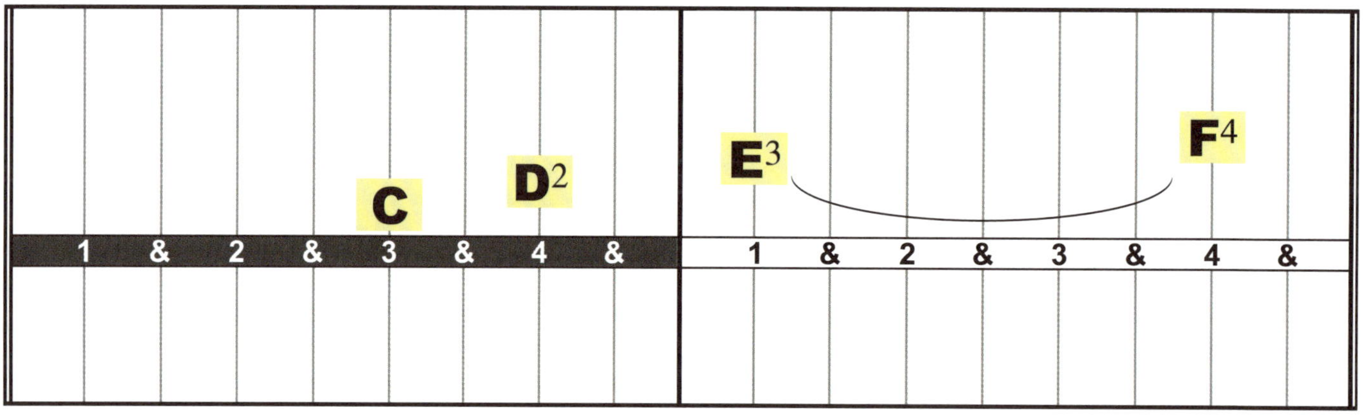

Please don't take my

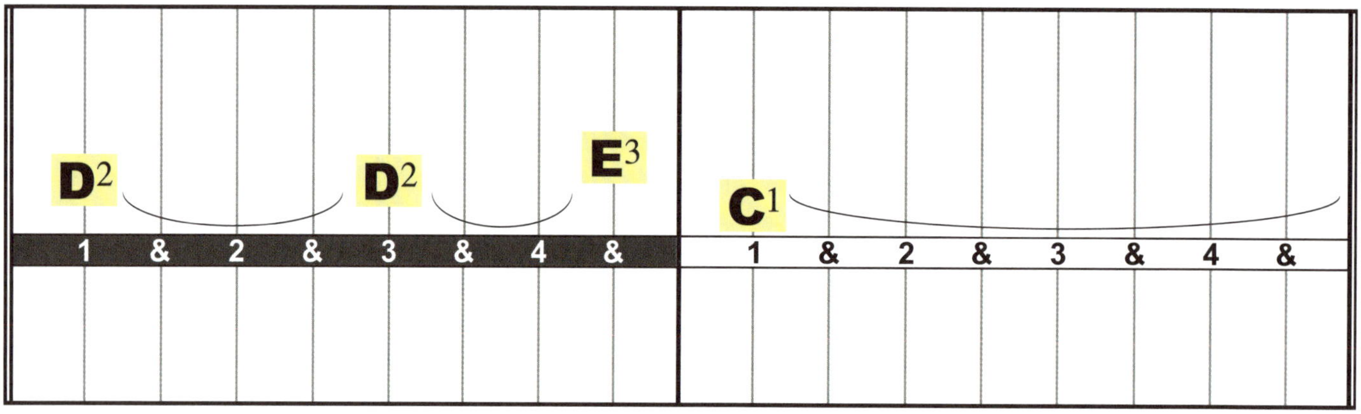

Sun - shine a - way

It's Raining, It's Pouring

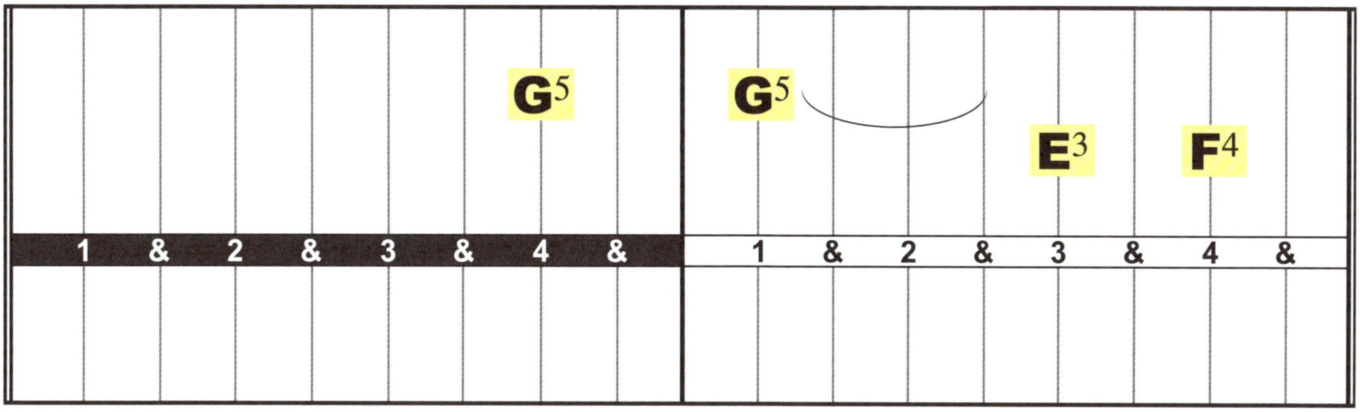

It's Rain — ing it's

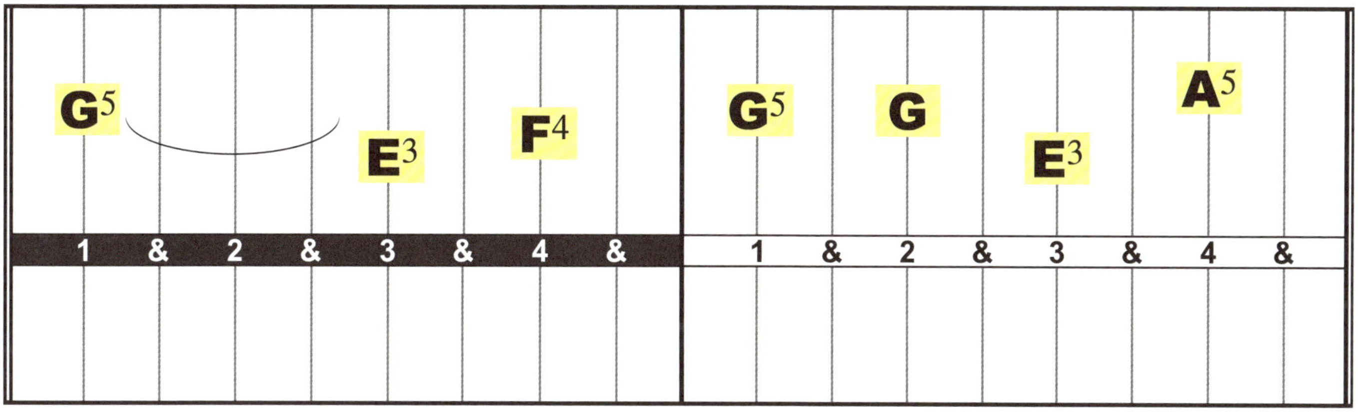

pour — ing the o — ld man is

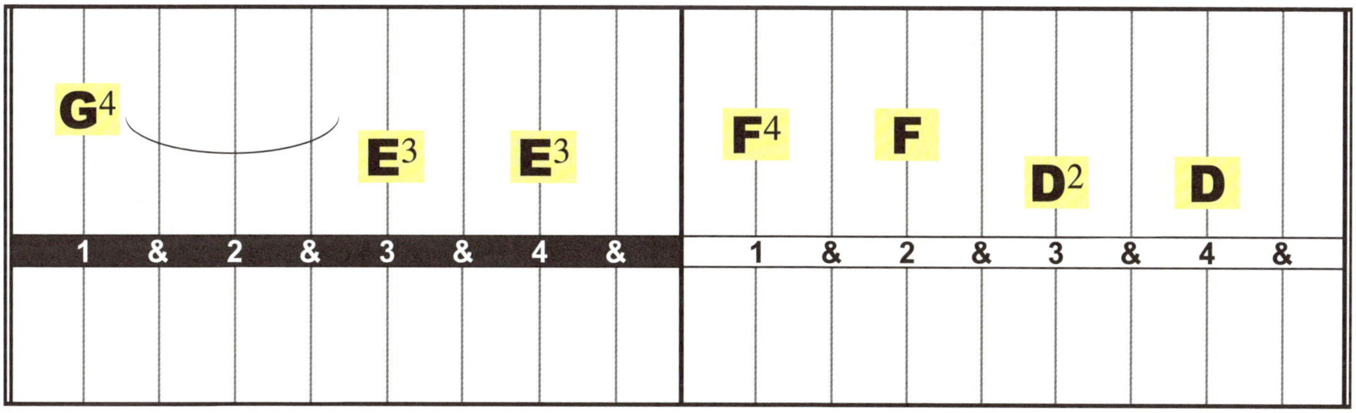

snor — ing. He bumped his head when he

F^{4}		F		D^{2}		D		G^{5}		F^{4}		E^{3}		D^{2}	
1	&	2	&	3	&	4	&	1	&	2	&	3	&	4	&
went		to		bed		and he		couldn't		get		up		in the	

E^{3}				C^{1}			
1	&	2	&	3	&	4	&
morn		—		ing _________________.			

Row, Row, Row your Boat

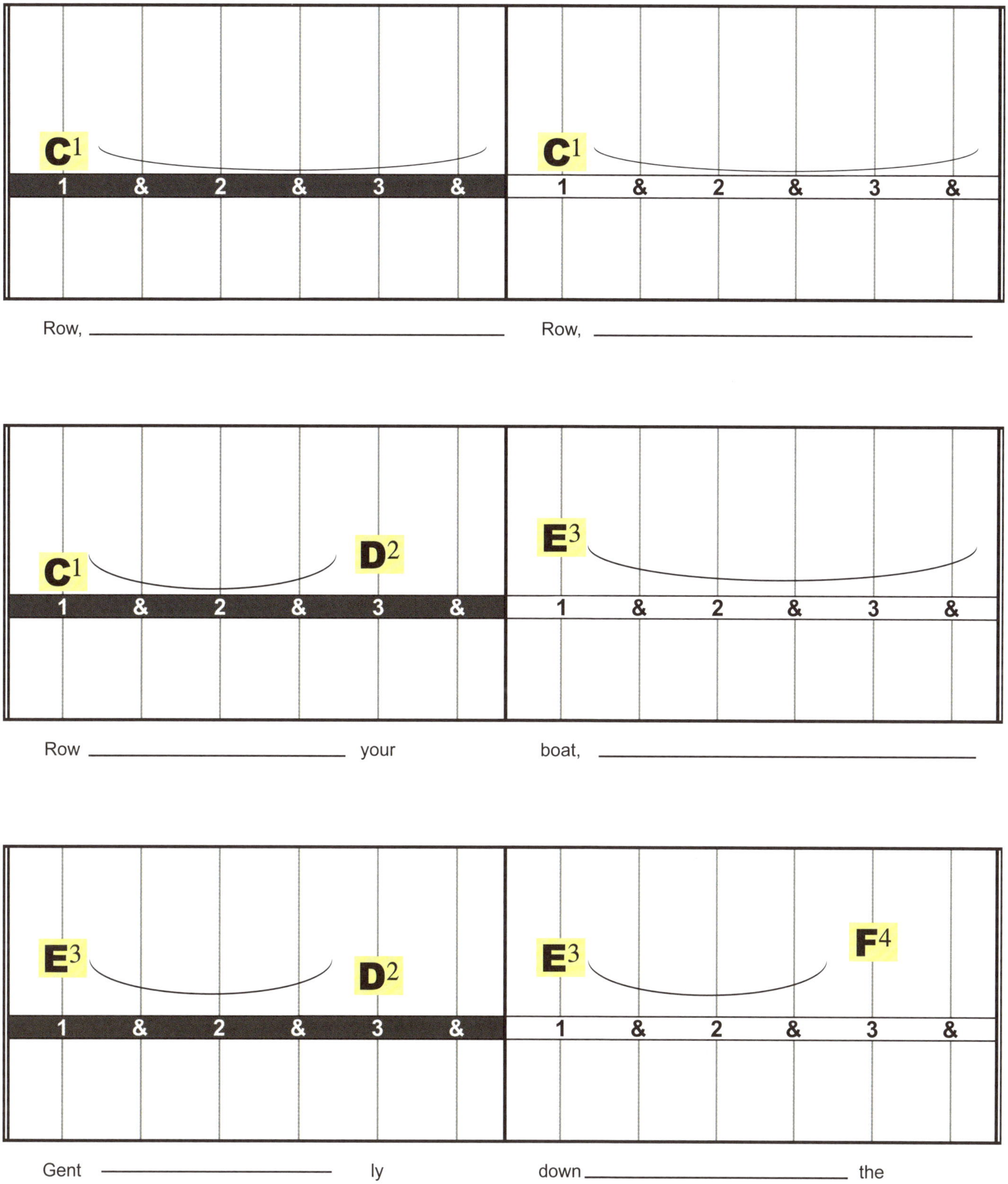

G^5						(G^5)					
1	&	2	&	3	&	1	&	2	&	3	&
stream											.

Left Hand Over (C^2 to C)

C^2		C		C		G^5		G		G	
1	&	2	&	3	&	1	&	2	&	3	&
Mer	-	ri	-	ly,		Mer	-	ri	-	ly,	

E^3		E		E		C^1		C		C	
1	&	2	&	3	&	1	&	2	&	3	&
Mer	-	ri	-	ly,		Mer	-	ri	-	ly	

G^5				F^4		E^3				D^2	
1	&	2	&	3	&	1	&	2	&	3	&

life ______________________ is   but ______________________ a

C^1						(C^1)					
1	&	2	&	3	&	1	&	2	&	3	&

dream ____ .

Ode to Joy

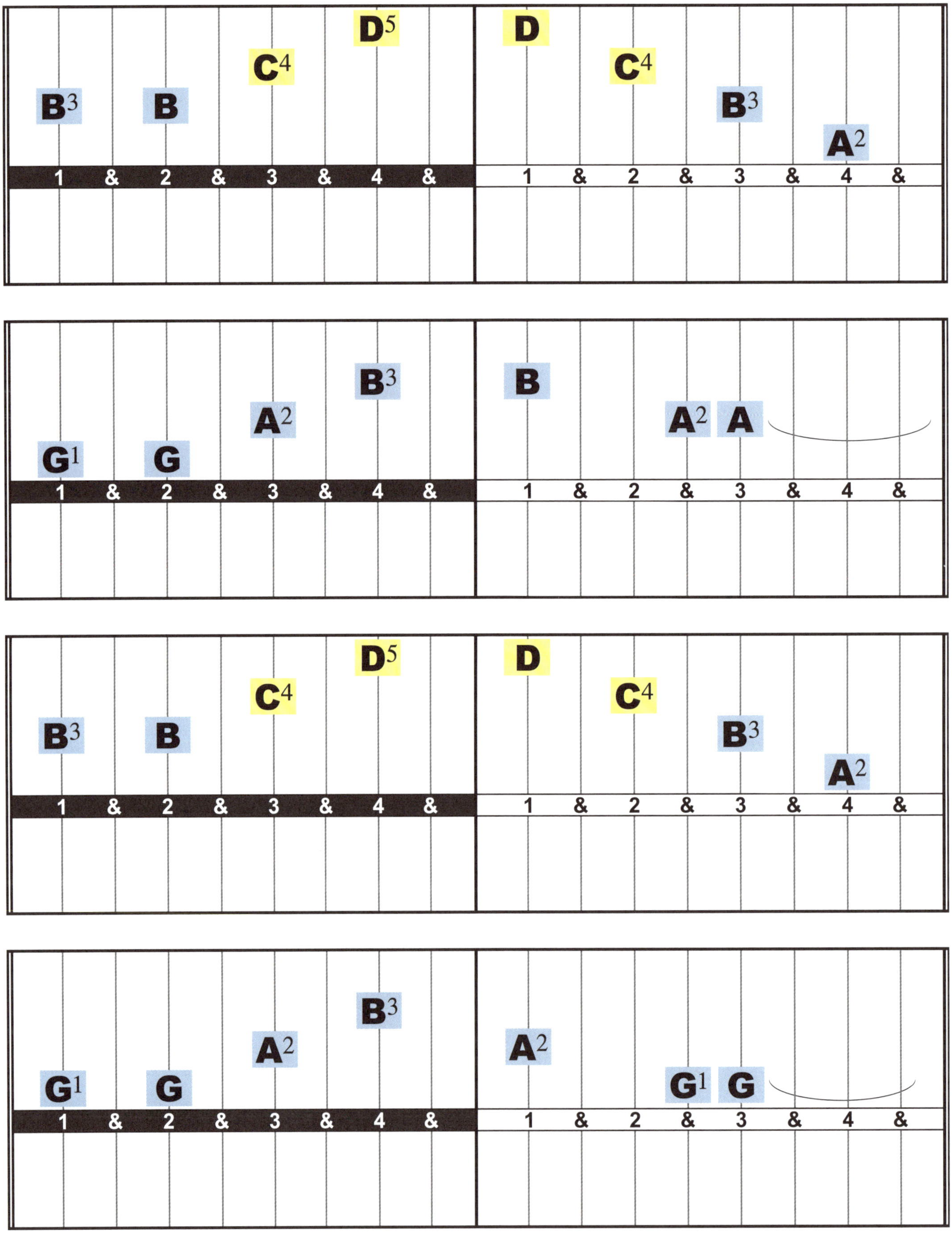
B3 B C4 D5 D C4 B3 A2
1 & 2 & 3 & 4 & 1 & 2 & 3 & 4 &
G1 G A2 B3 B A2 A
1 & 2 & 3 & 4 & 1 & 2 & 3 & 4 &
B3 B C4 D5 D C4 B3 A2
1 & 2 & 3 & 4 & 1 & 2 & 3 & 4 &
G1 G A2 B3 A2 G1 G
1 & 2 & 3 & 4 & 1 & 2 & 3 & 4 &

Baby Shark

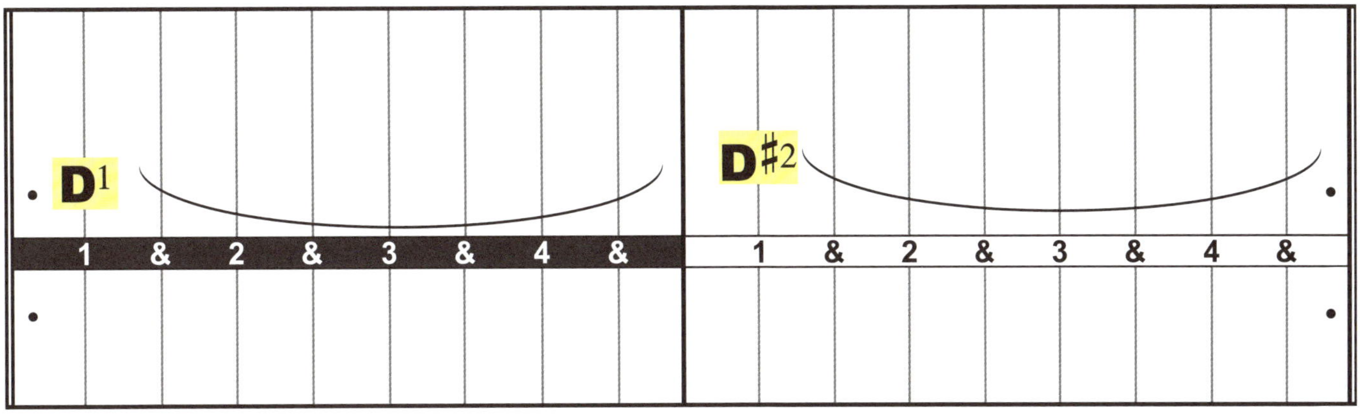

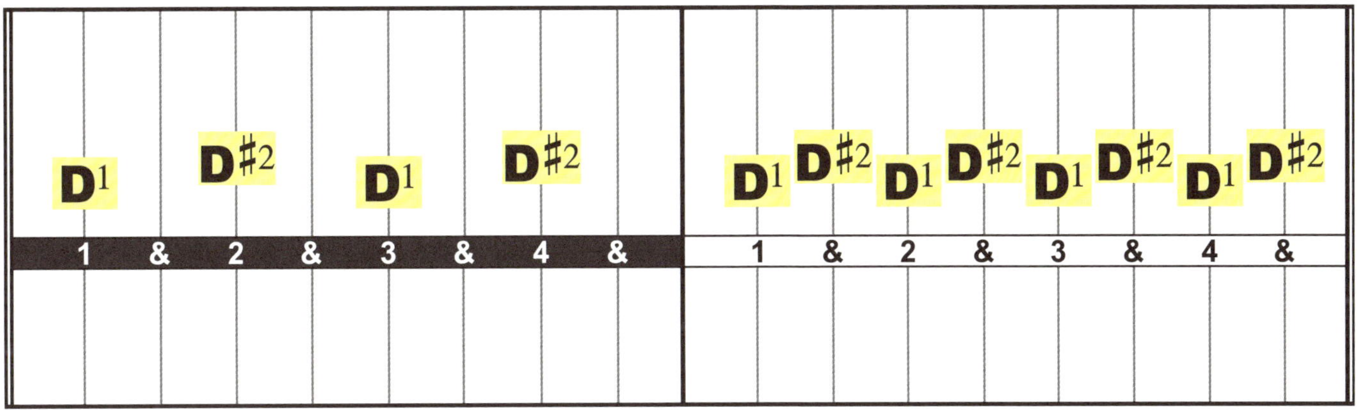

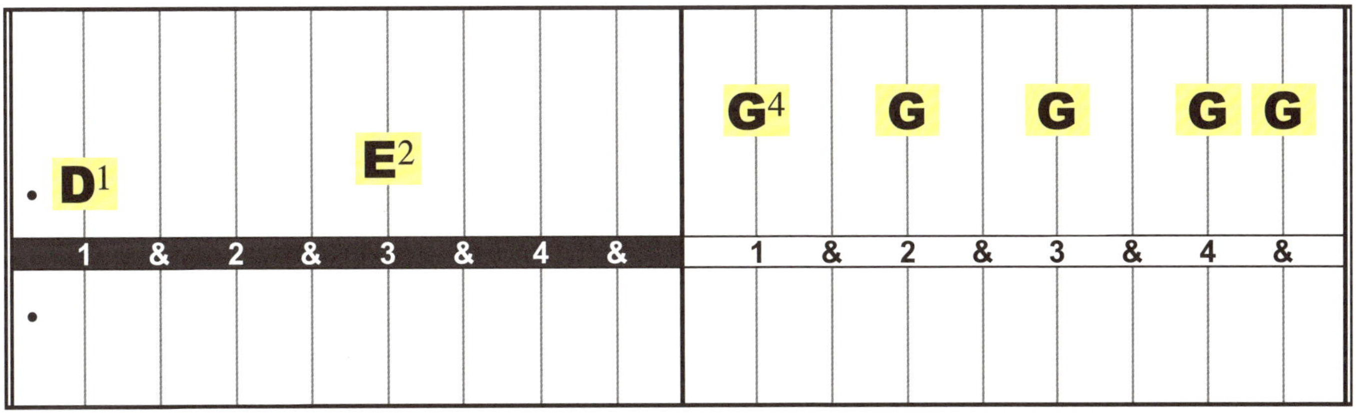

Ba — by shark do do do - do

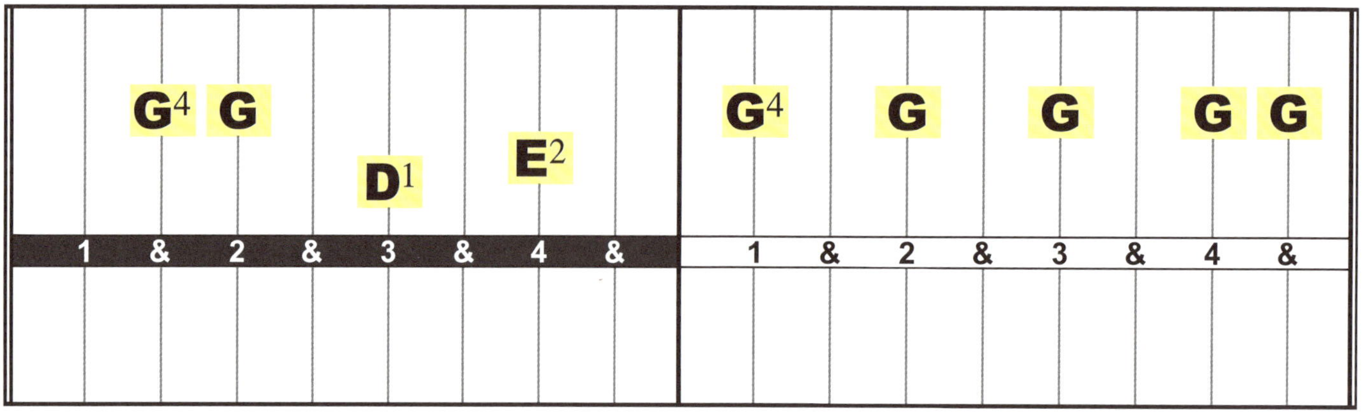

do - do Ba — by shark do do do - do

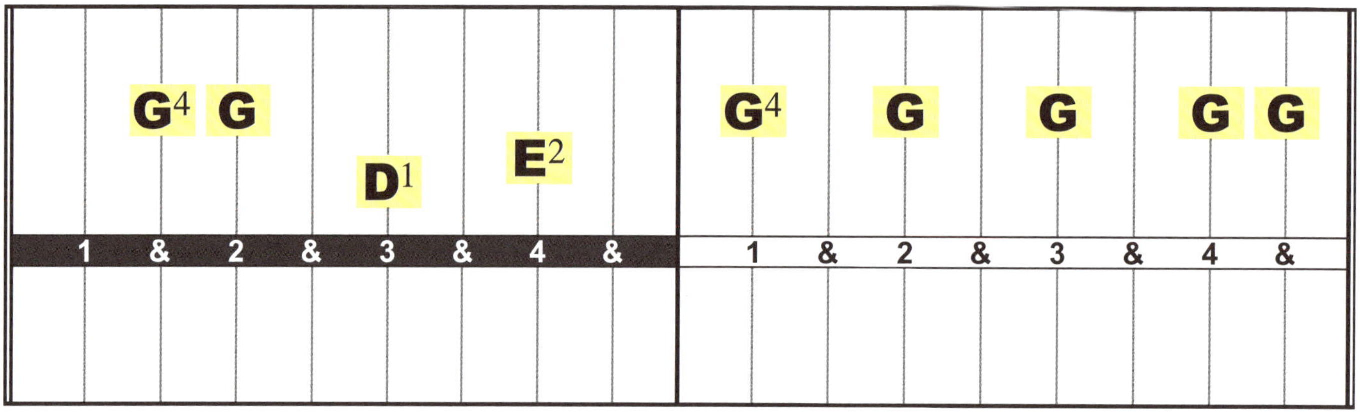

do - do Ba — by shark do do do - do

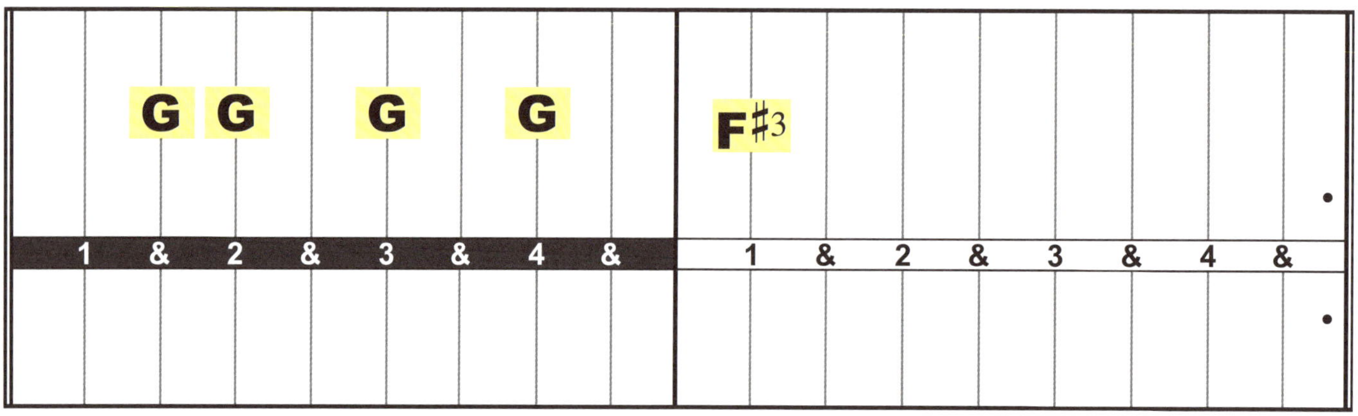

do - do Ba — by shark.

London Bridge

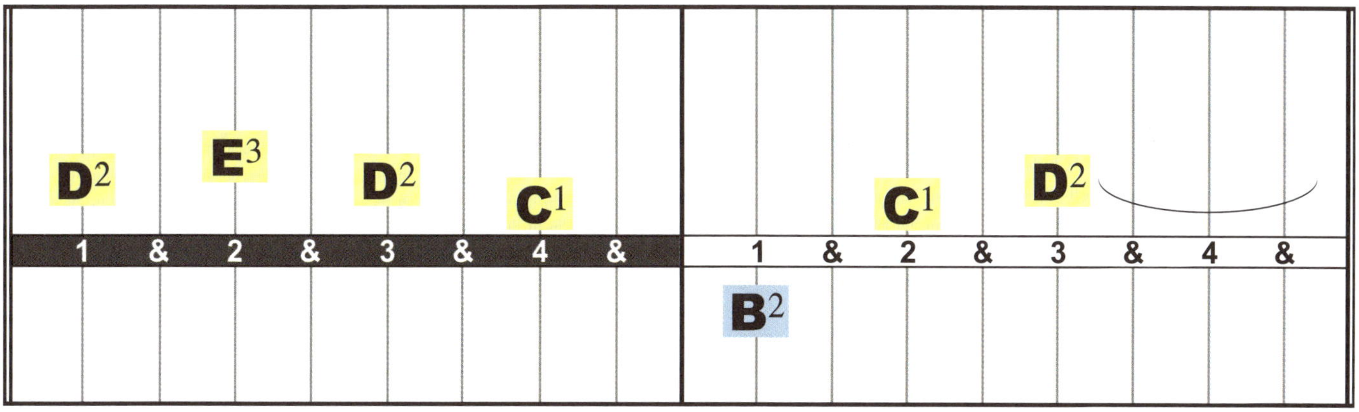

Lon - don bridge is fall - ing down, ________

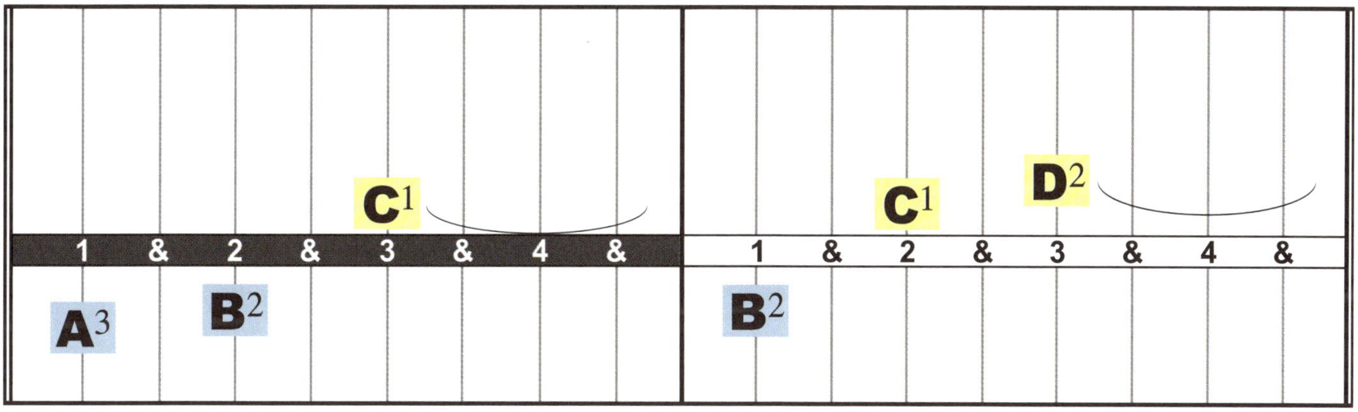

fall - ing down, ________ fall - ing down. ________

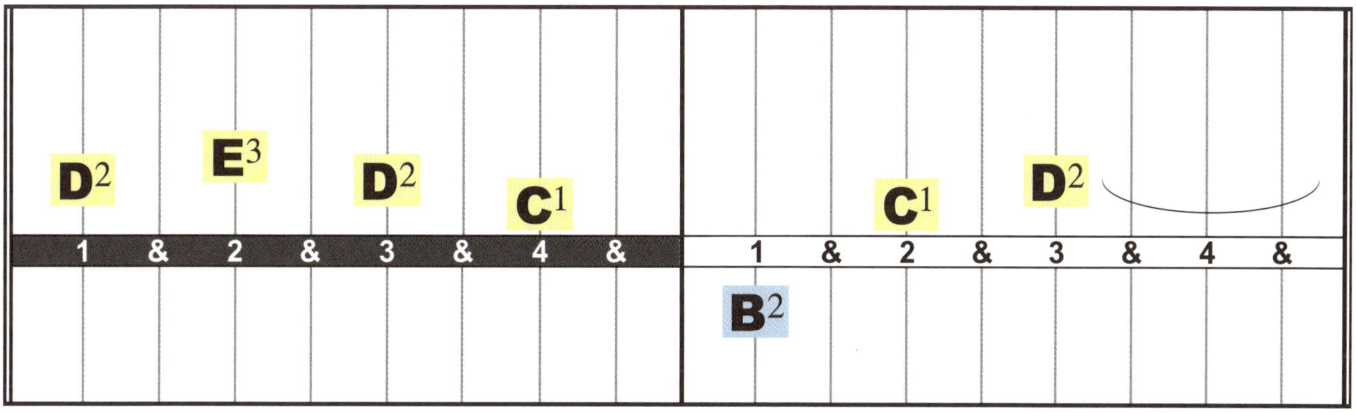

Lon - don bridge is fall - ing down. ________

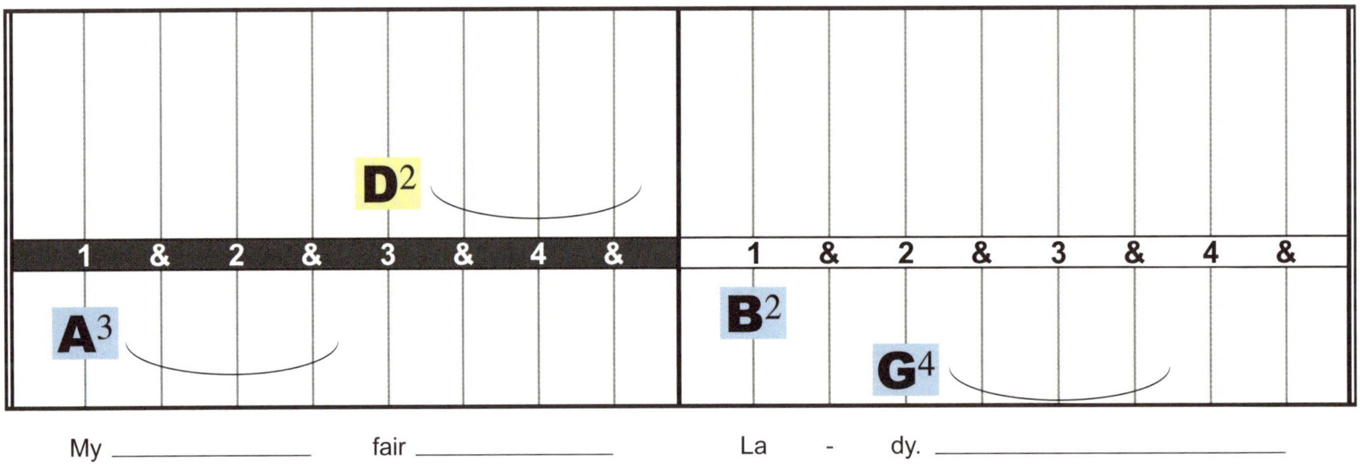

D2
1 & 2 & 3 & 4 &
1 & 2 & 3 & 4 &
A3
B2
G4
My
fair
La
-
dy.

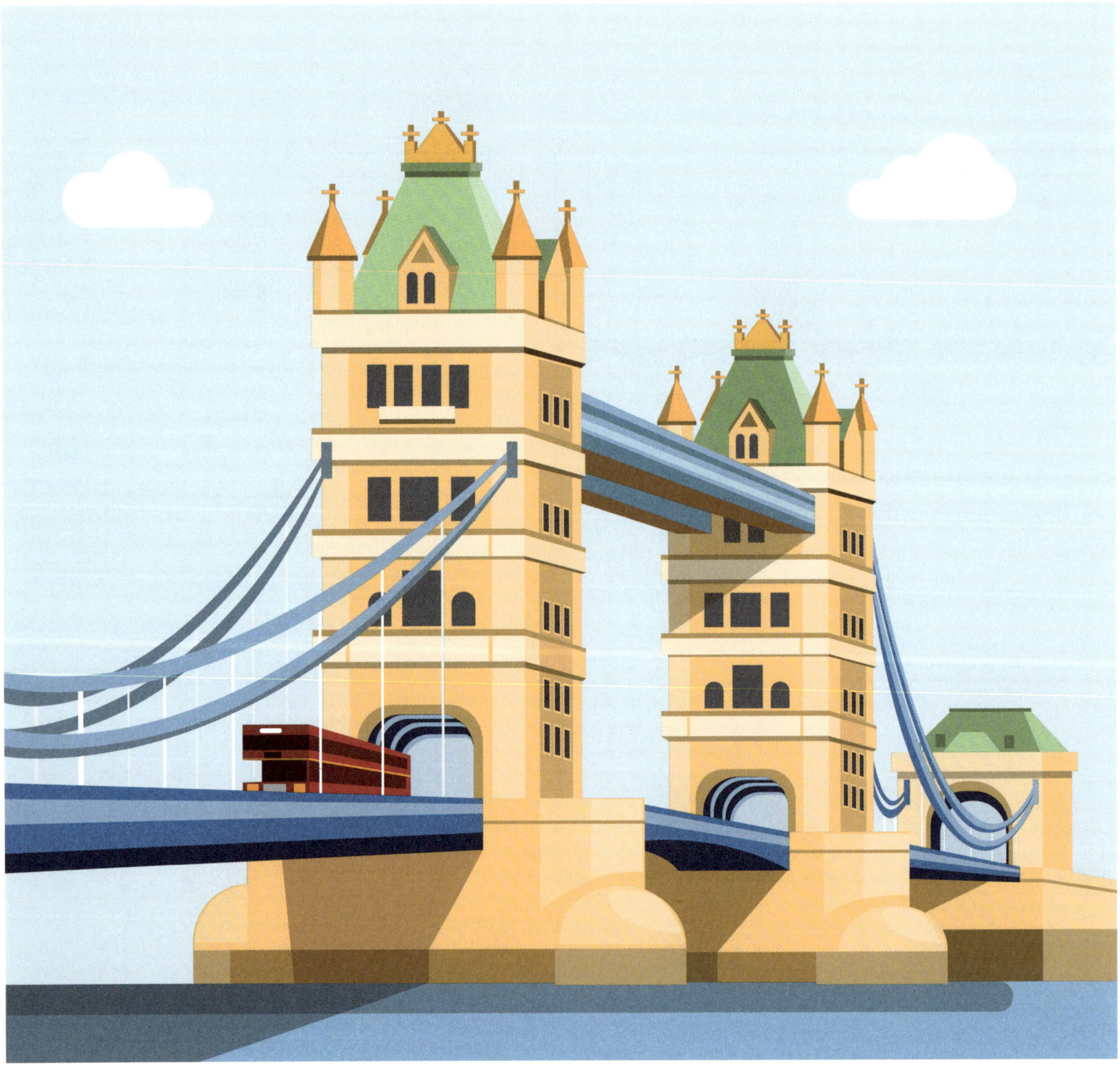

Jolly Old Saint Nick

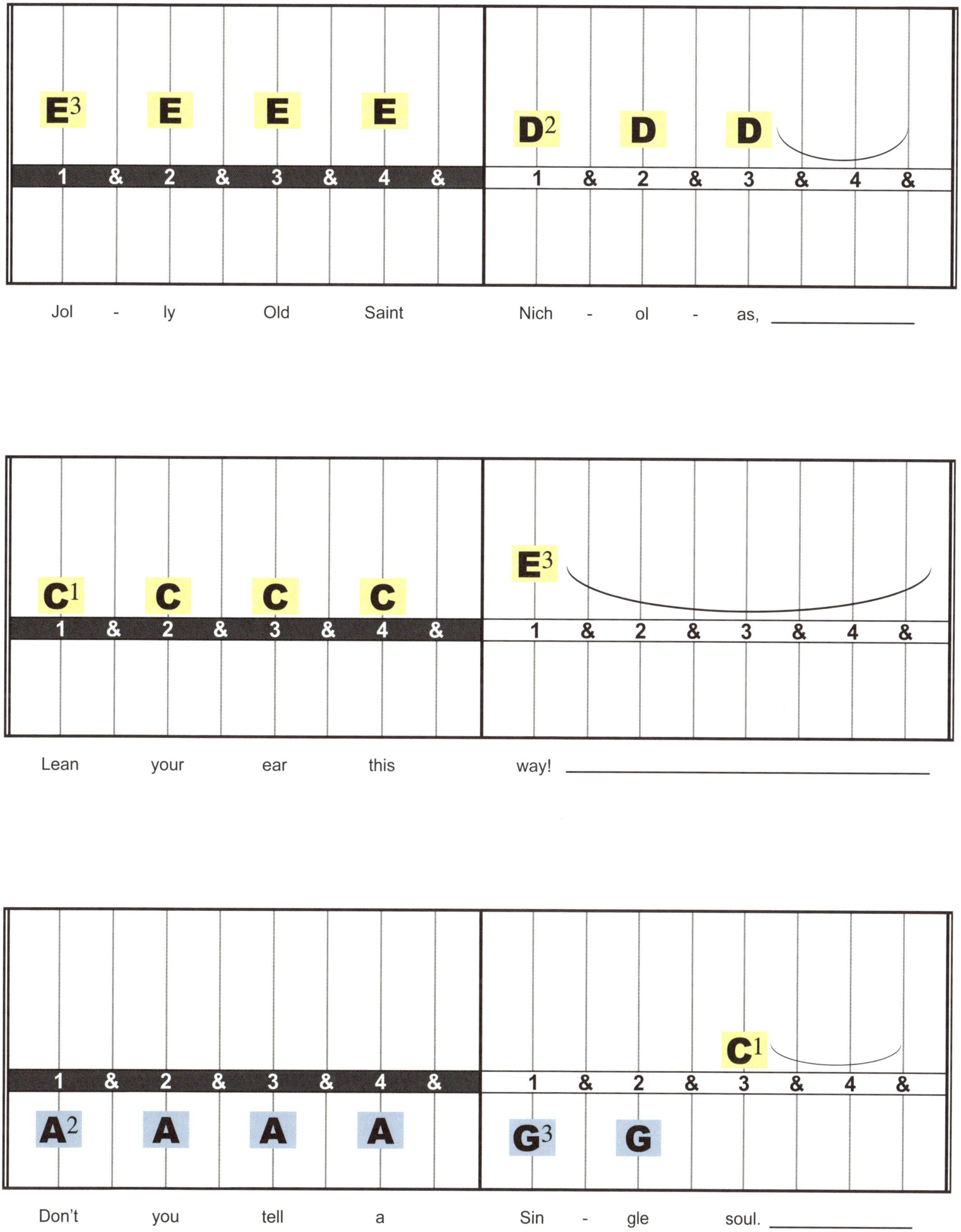

1	&	2	&	3	&	4	&	1	&	2	&	3	&	4	&
D^2		C^1		D^2		E^3		D^2							
What		I'm		going		to		say;							

1	&	2	&	3	&	4	&	1	&	2	&	3	&	4	&
E^3		E		E		E		D^2		D		D			
Christ	-	mas		eve		is		Com	-	ing		soon;			

1	&	2	&	3	&	4	&	1	&	2	&	3	&	4	&
C^1		C		C		C		E^3							
Now,		you		dear		old		man,							

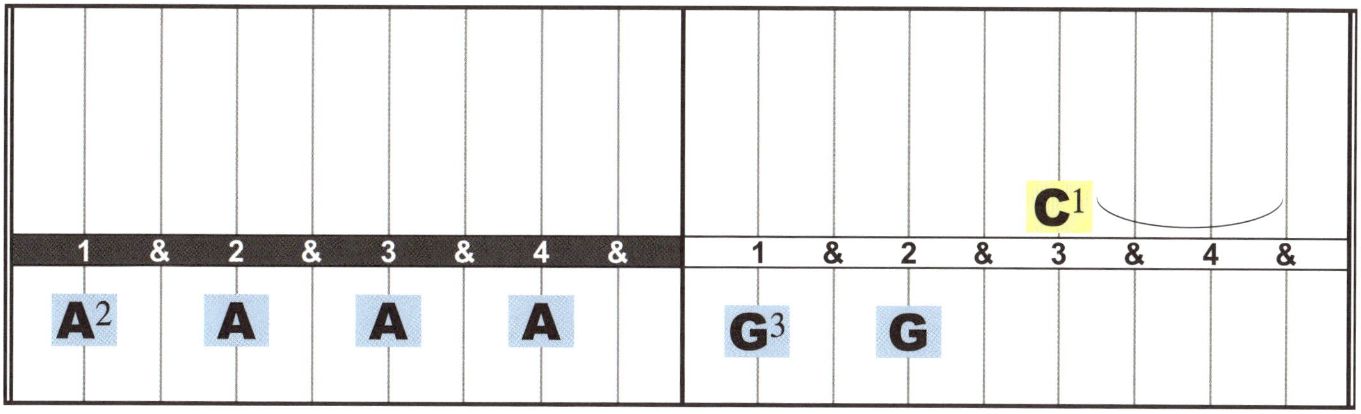

Whis - per what you'll bring to me. ________

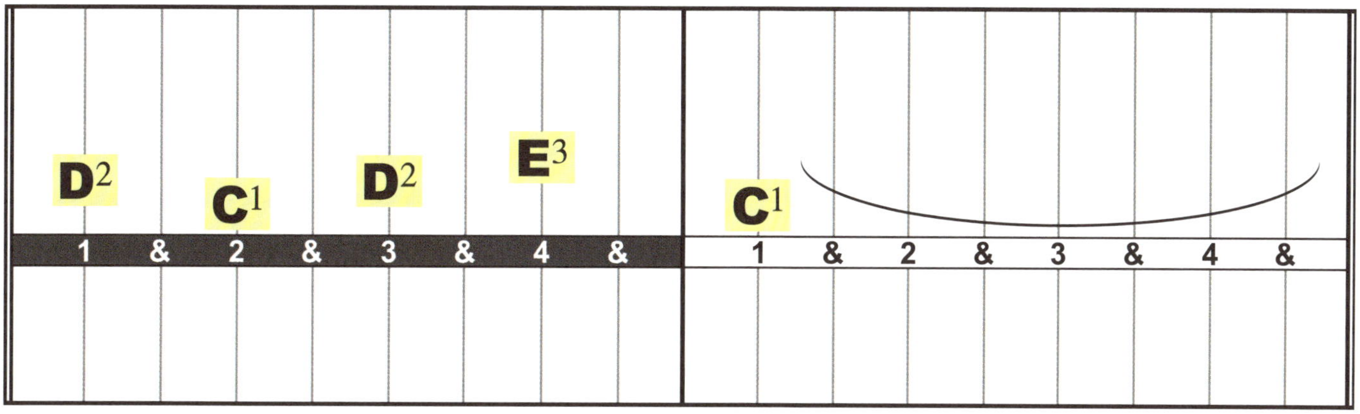

Tell me if you can. ________

Old McDonald

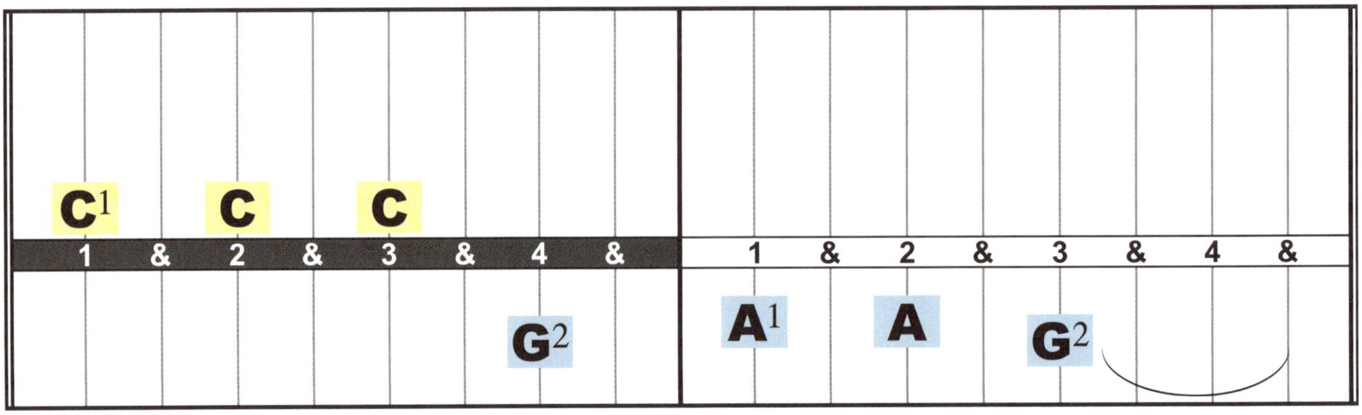

Old Mac - don - ald had a farm,

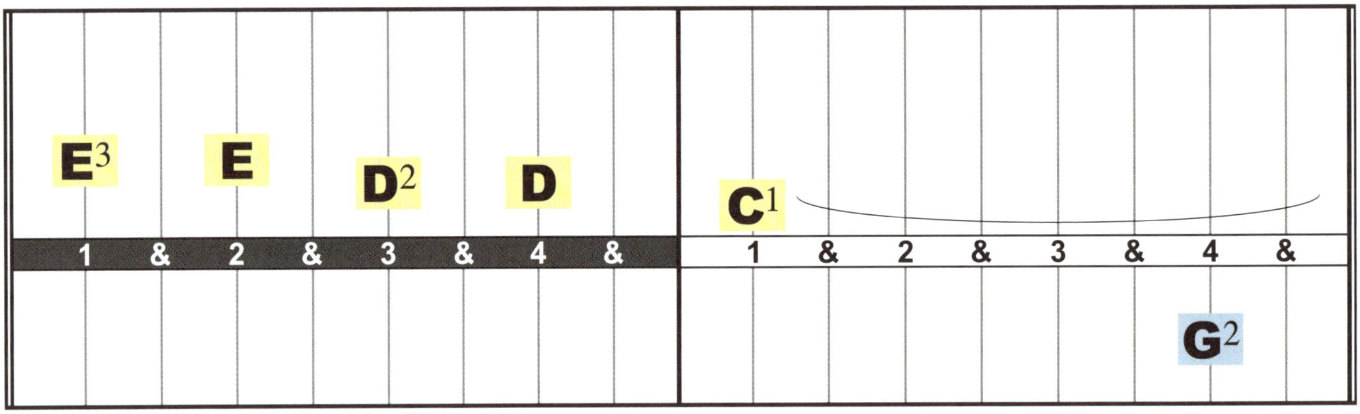

E - I - E - I - Oh ______________________

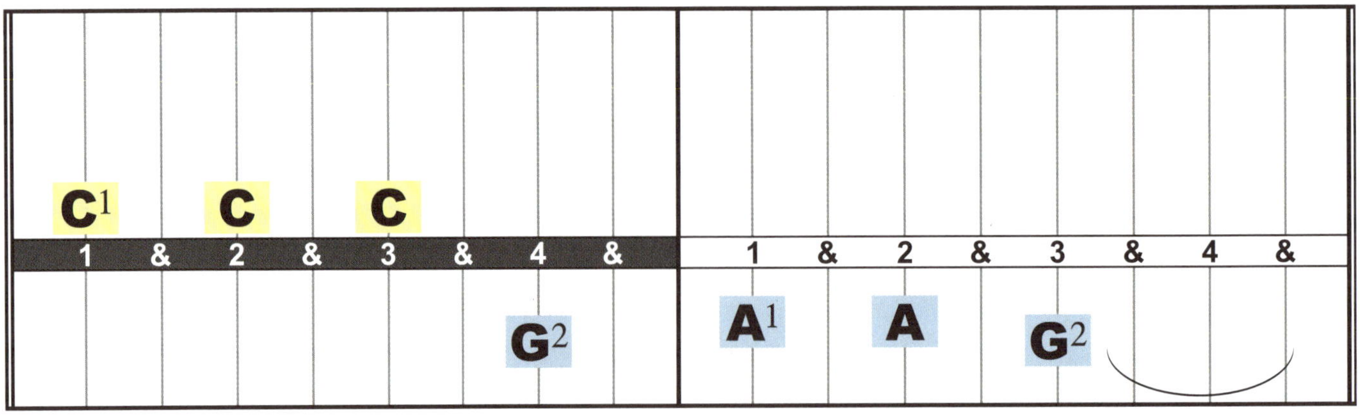

On that farm he had a pig,

E3		E		D2		D		C1 (held)							
1	&	2	&	3	&	4	&	1	&	2	&	3	&	4	&
E	-	I	-	E	-	I	-	Oh ___							

The Wheels on the Bus

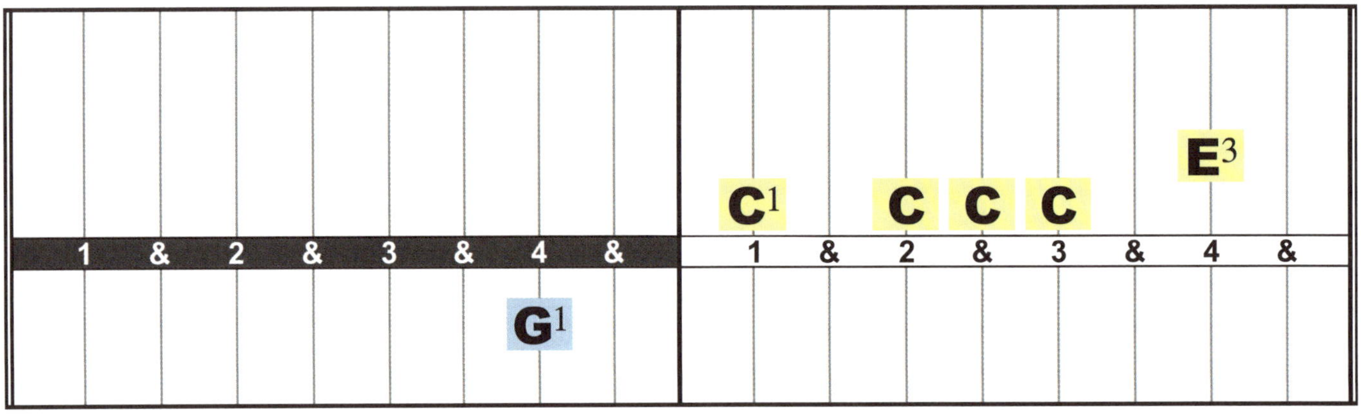

The wheels on the bus go

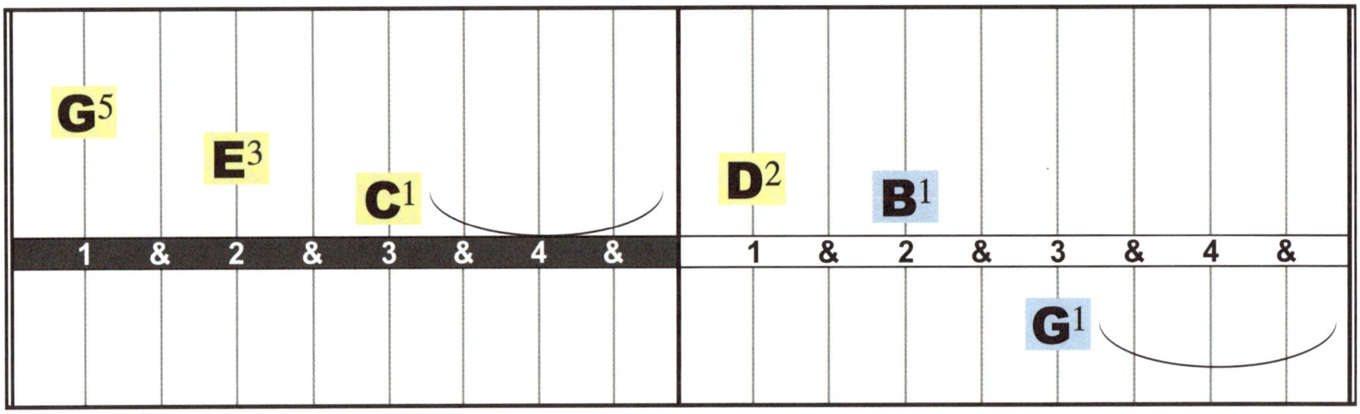

Round and round. Round and round ________

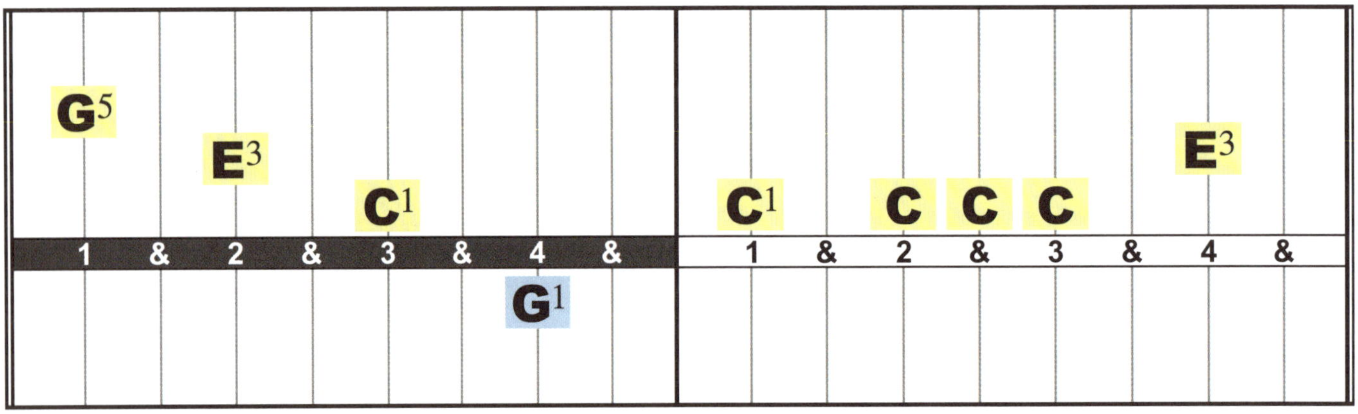

Round and round. The wheels on the bus go

G^5		E^3		C^1				D^2							
1	&	2	&	3	&	4	&	1	&	2	&	3	&	4	&
												G^1		G	
Round		and		round ______				All ______				through		the	

C^1					
1	&	2	&	3	&
town.					

Surprise Symphony

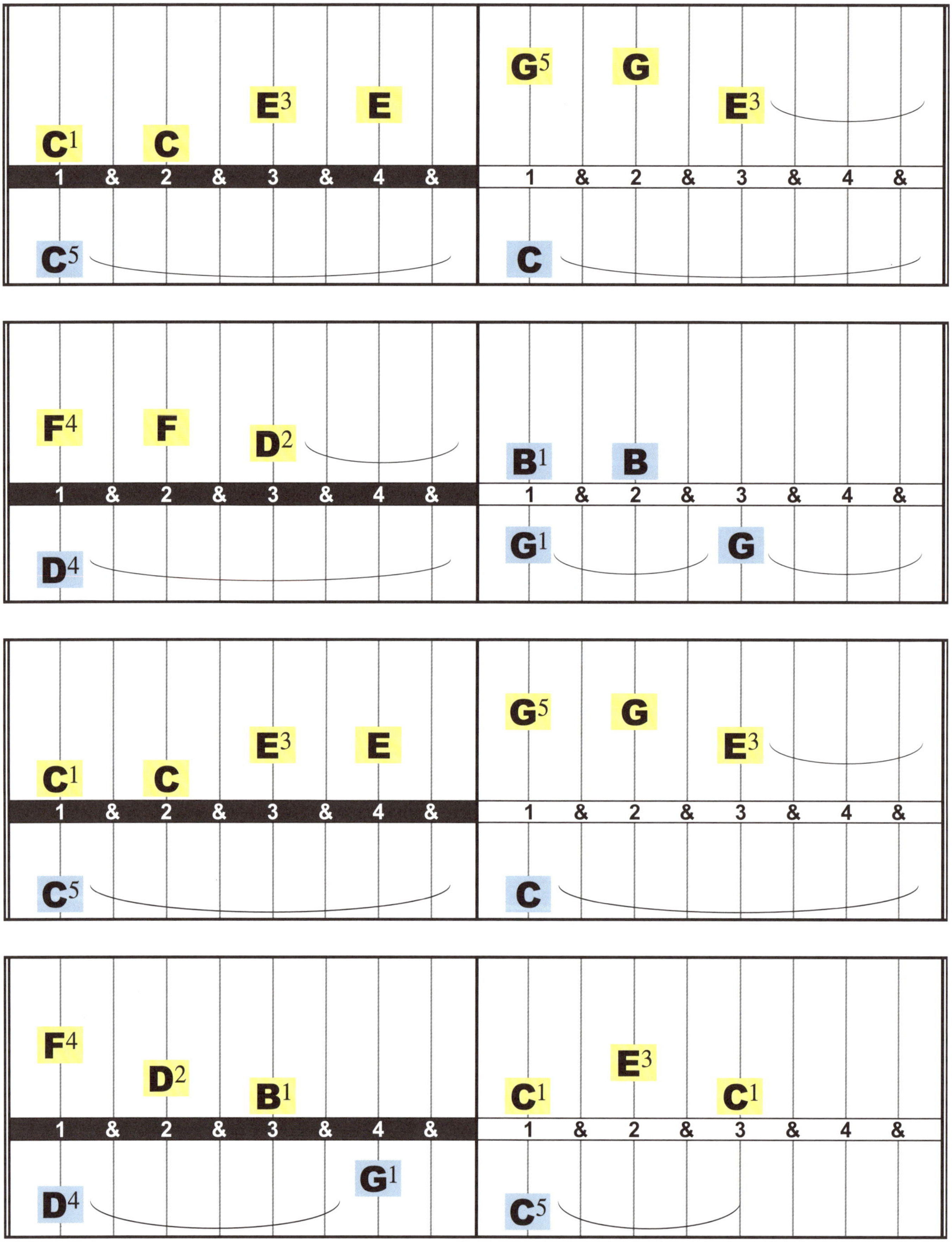

Bingo

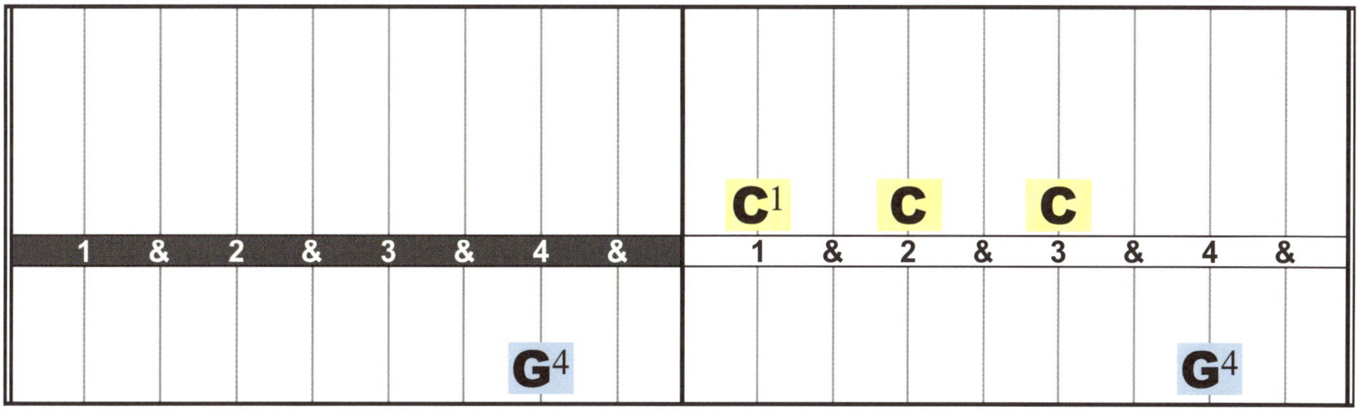

There was a farmer who

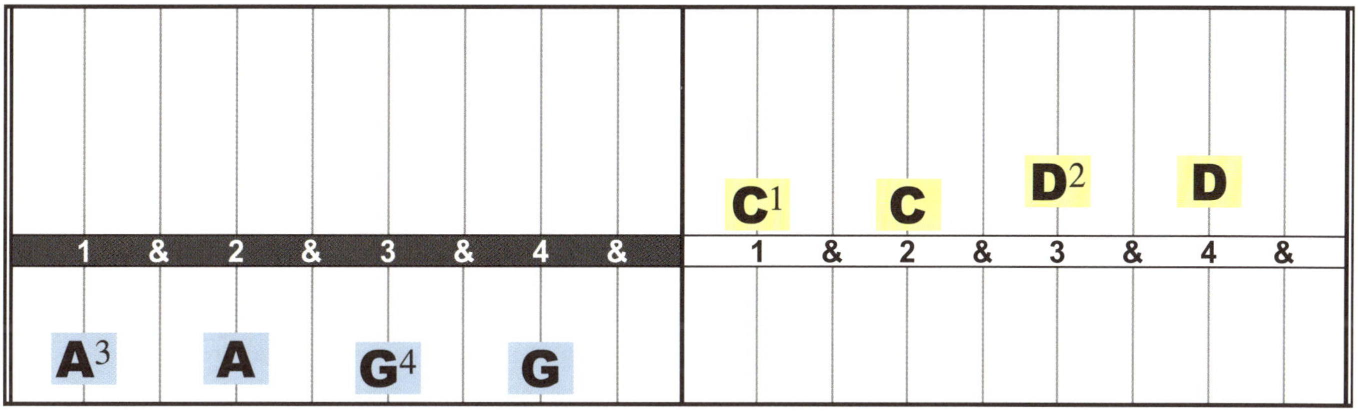

had a dog, and Bin - go was his

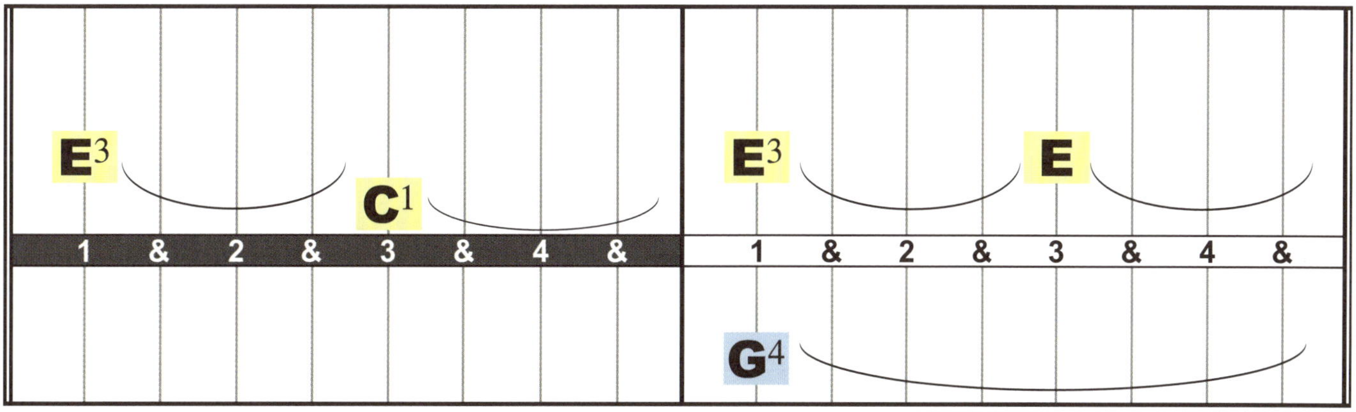

name ________ o ________ B ________ I ________

F^4		F		F				D^2				D			
1	&	2	&	3	&	4	&	1	&	2	&	3	&	4	&
A^3								B^2							

N G O ________ B ________ I ________

E^3		E		E				C^1				C			
1	&	2	&	3	&	4	&	1	&	2	&	3	&	4	&
C^1															

N G O ________ B ________ I ________

D^2		D		D		C^1									
1	&	2	&	3	&	4	&	1	&	2	&	3	&	4	&
F^5								B^2		G^4		A^3		B^2	

N G O, and Bin go was his

1	&	2	&	3	&	4	&
C^1				C			

name ________ o!

We Wish You a Merry Christmas

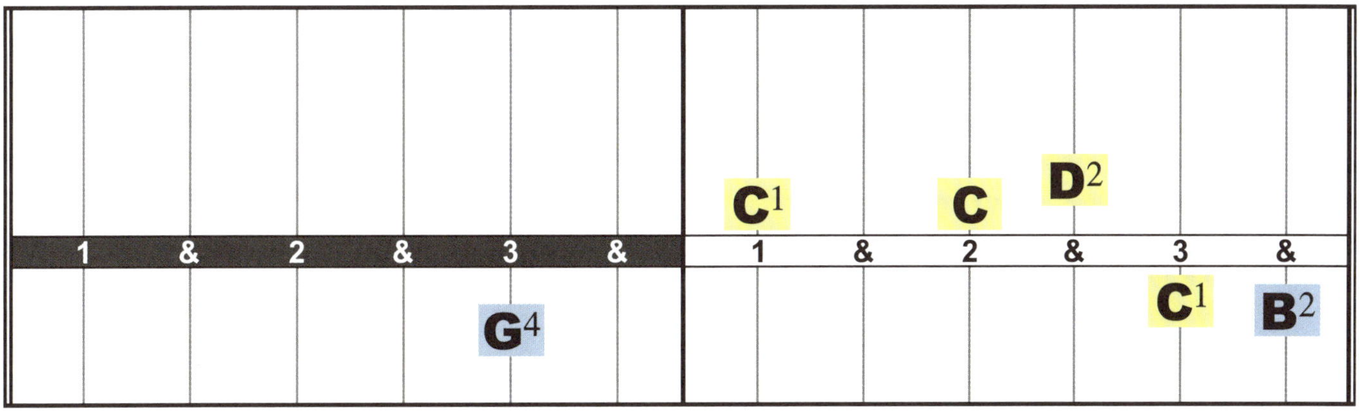

We wish you a mer - ry

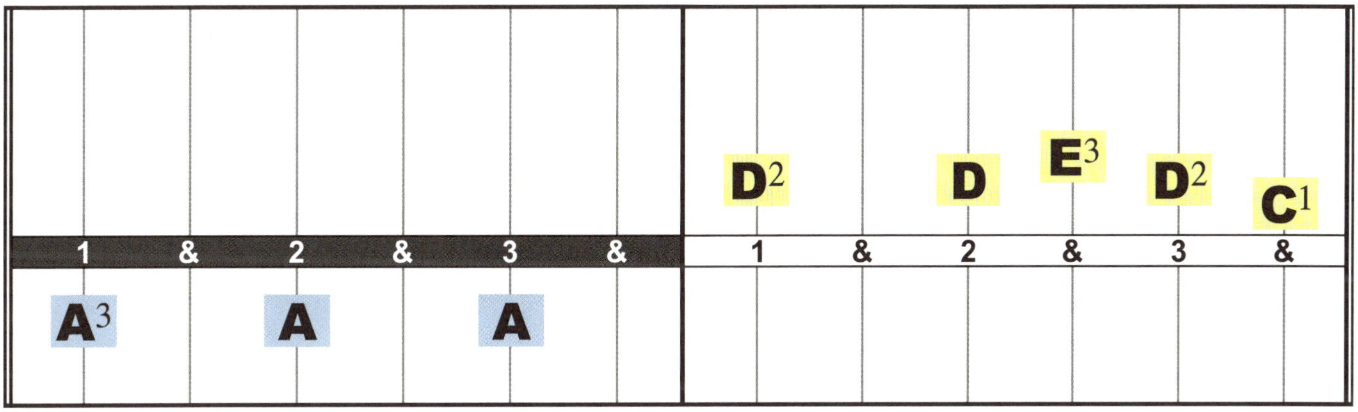

Christ - mas. We wish you a mer - ry

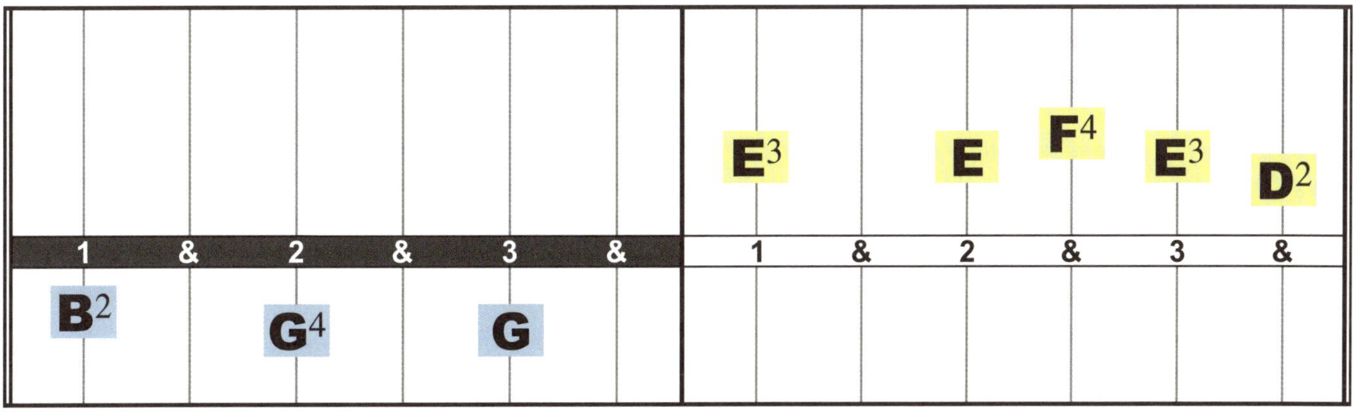

Christ - mas. We wish you a mer - ry

								D[2]			
1	&	2	&	3	&	1	&	2	&	3	&
C[1]		A[3]		G[4]	G	A[3]				B[2]	
Christ	-	mas		and	a	Hap	-	py		New	

1	&	2	&	3	&
C[1]					
Year!					

This Land is Your Land

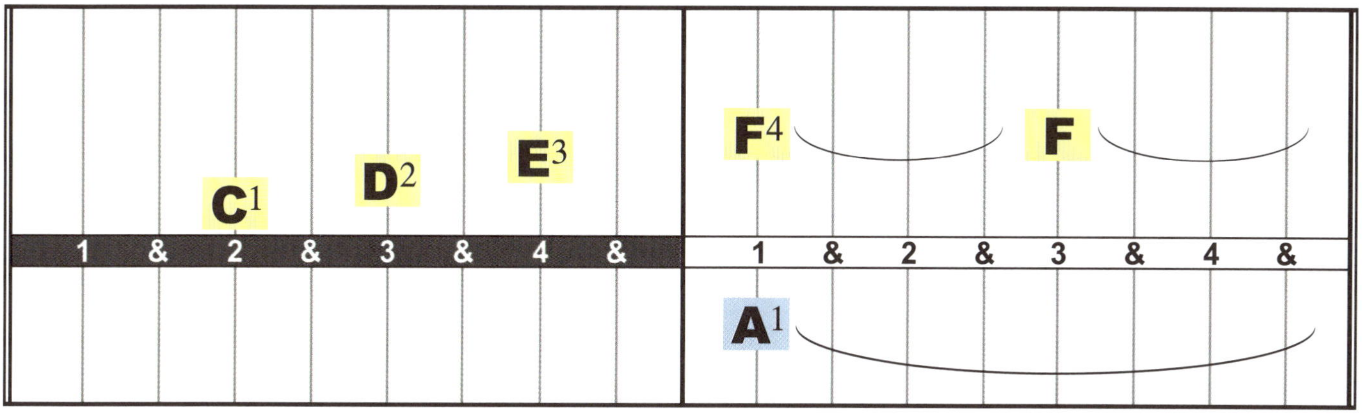

This Land is your land,

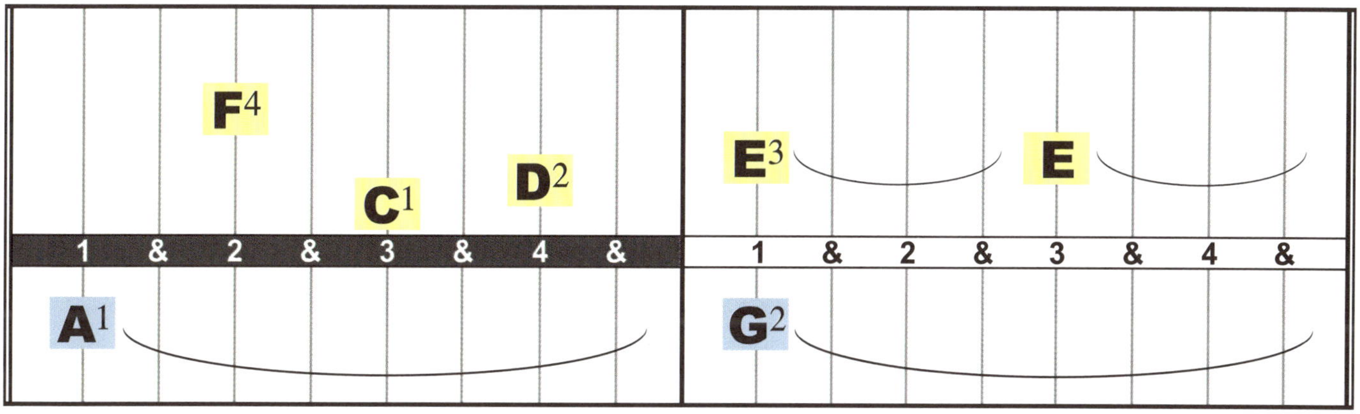

This land is my land

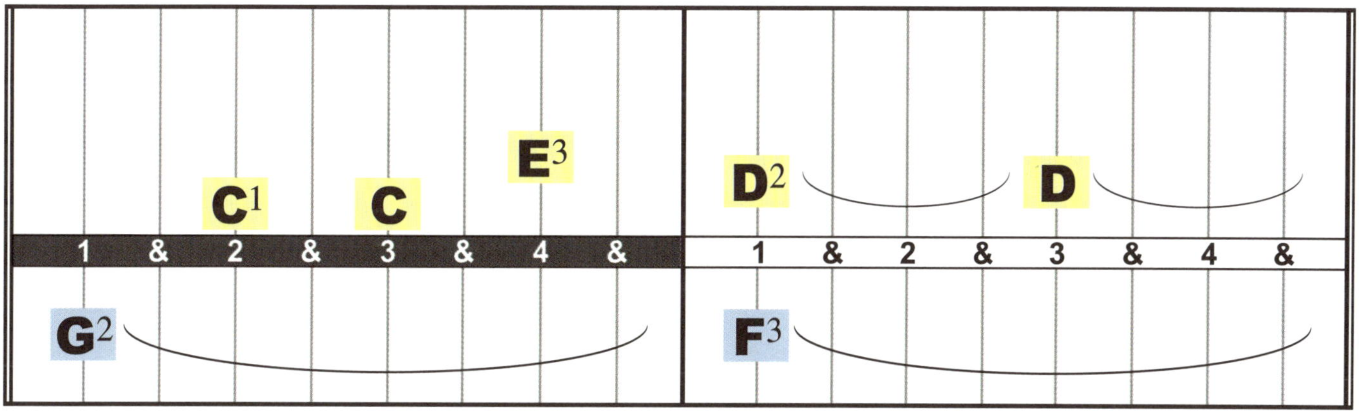

From Ca - li - for - nia

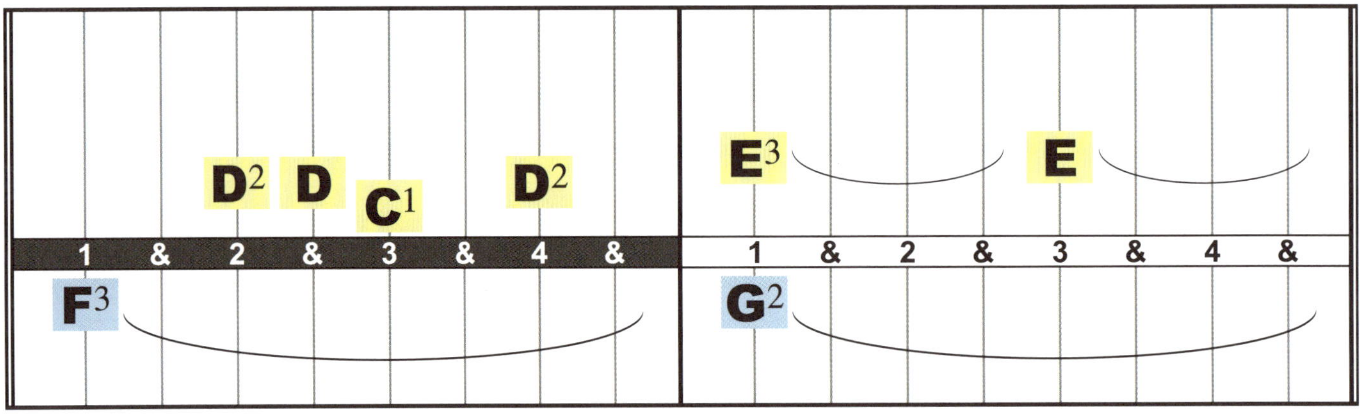

To the New York Is - land.

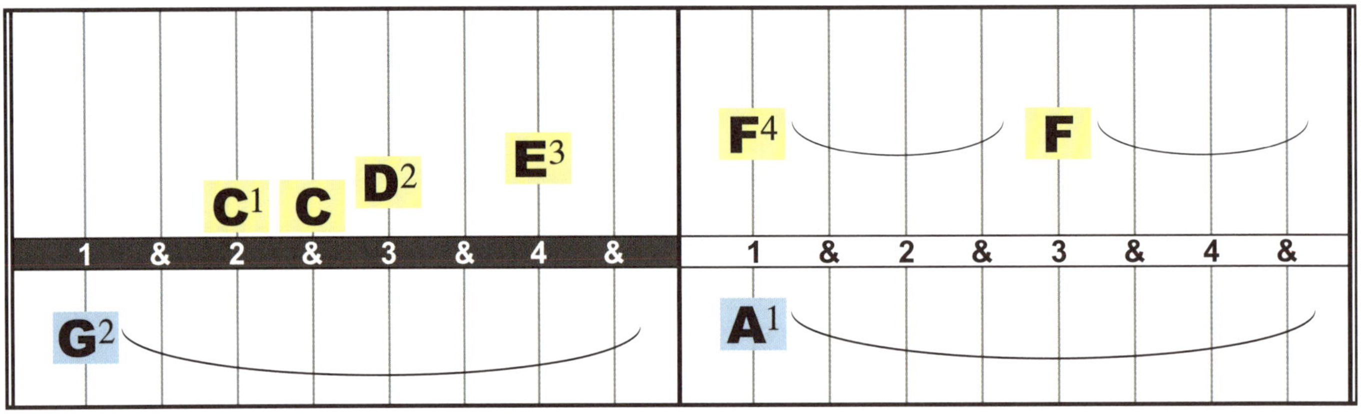

From the Red - wood Fo - rests,

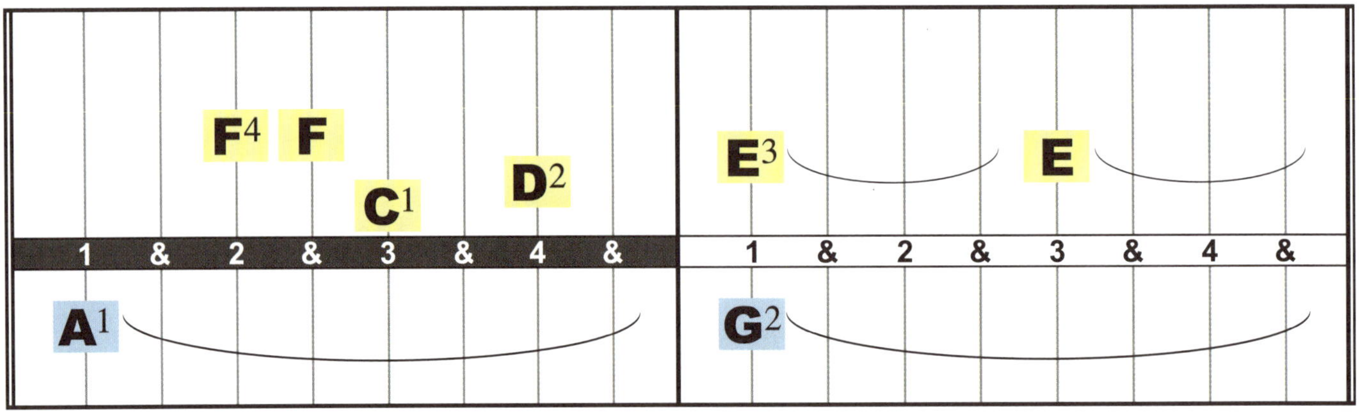

To the Gulf Stream Wa - ters

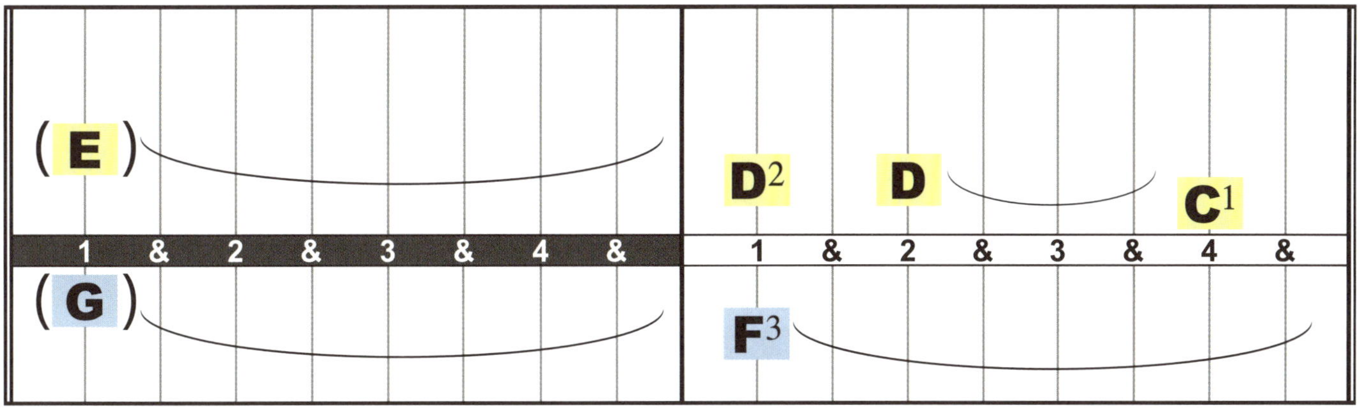

This land was

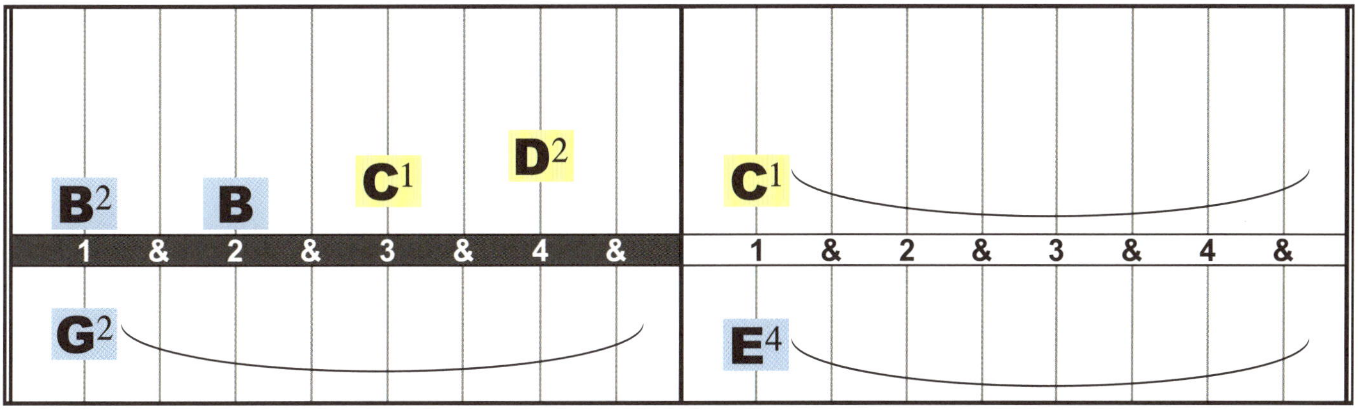

made for you and me.

Happy Birthday

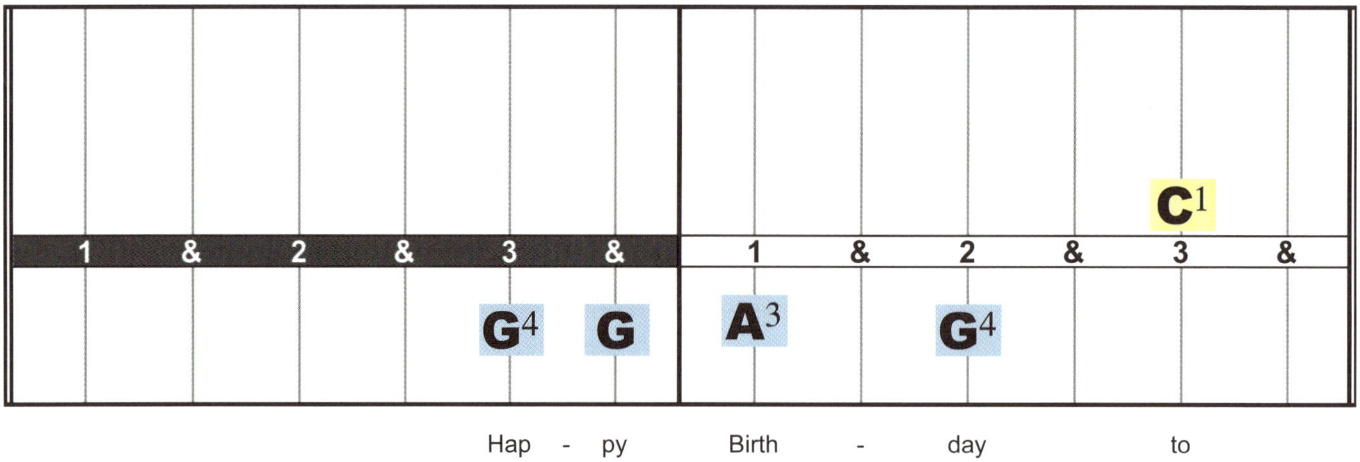

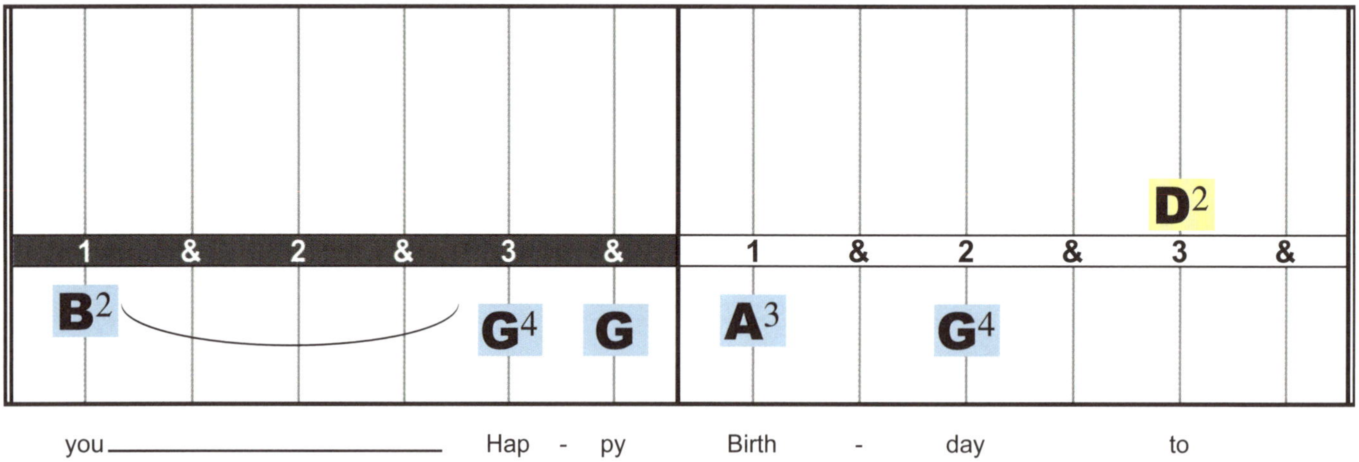

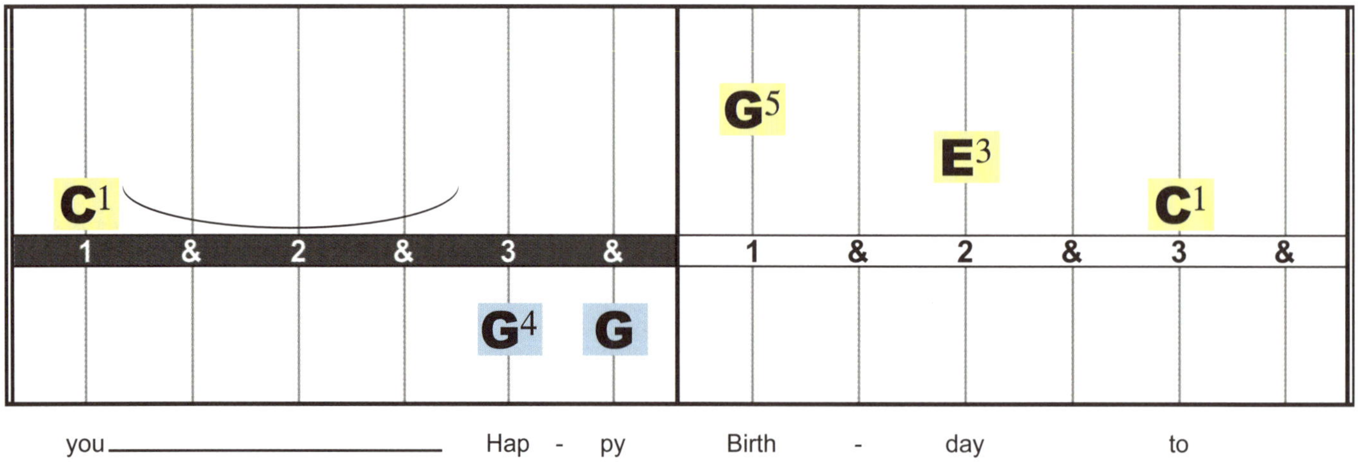

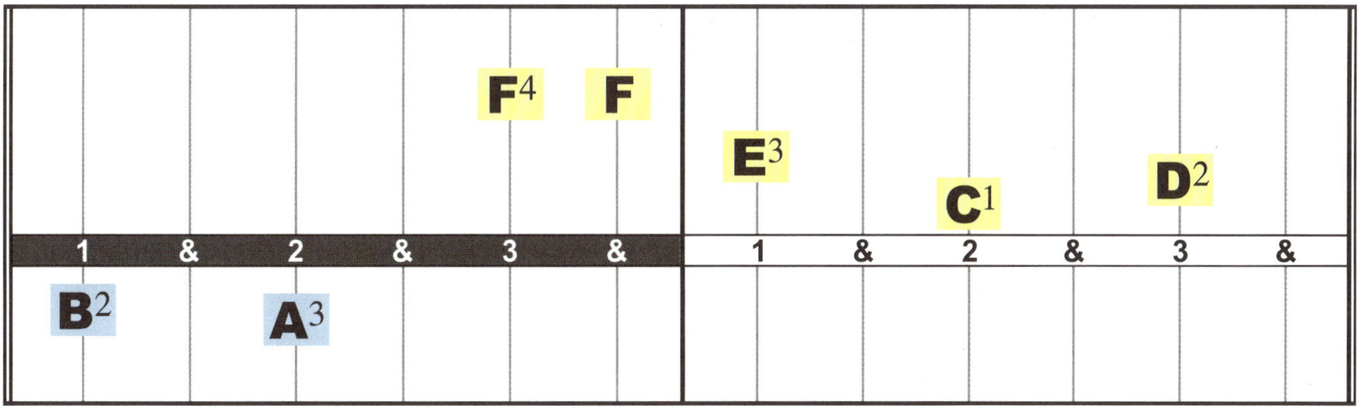

(INSERT NAME) Hap - py Birth - day to

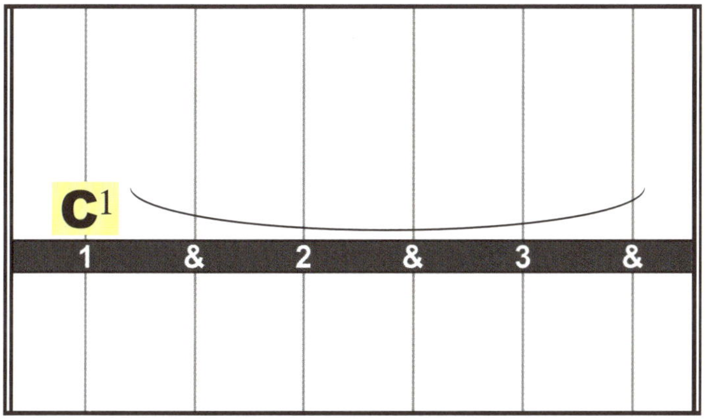

you____

Do You Know the Muffin Man

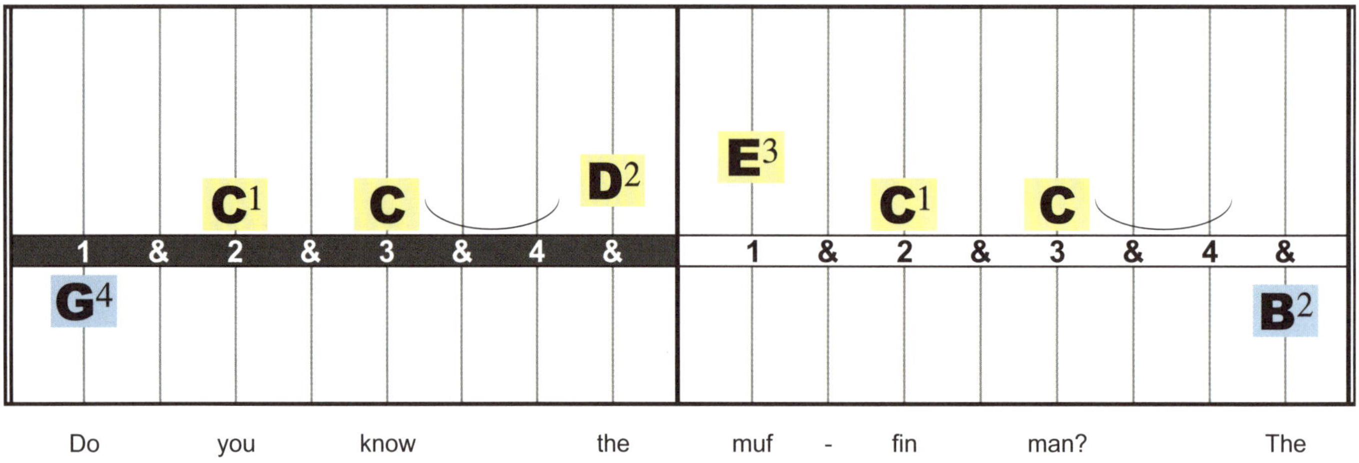

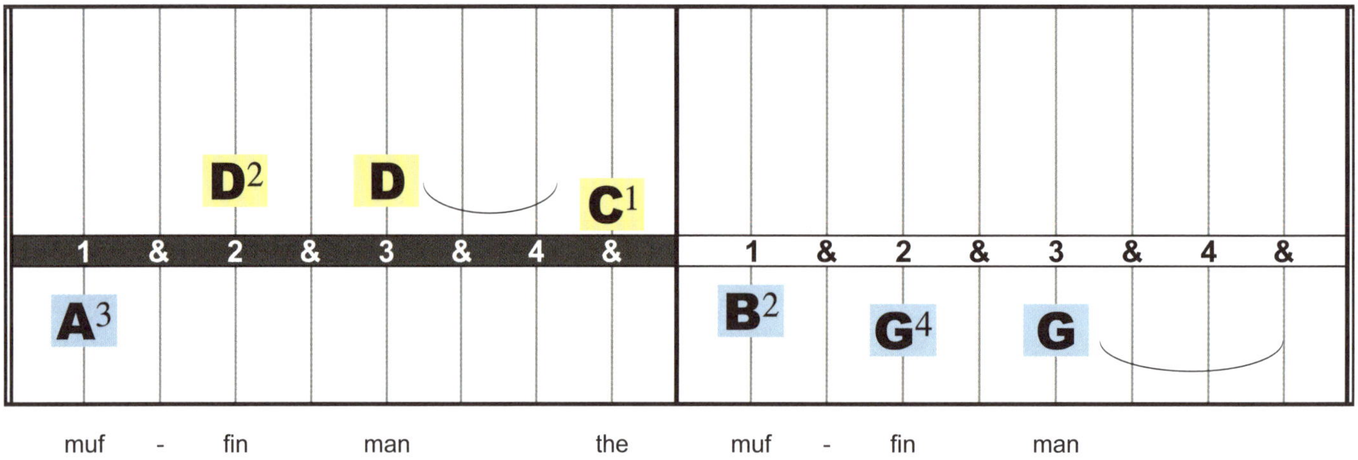

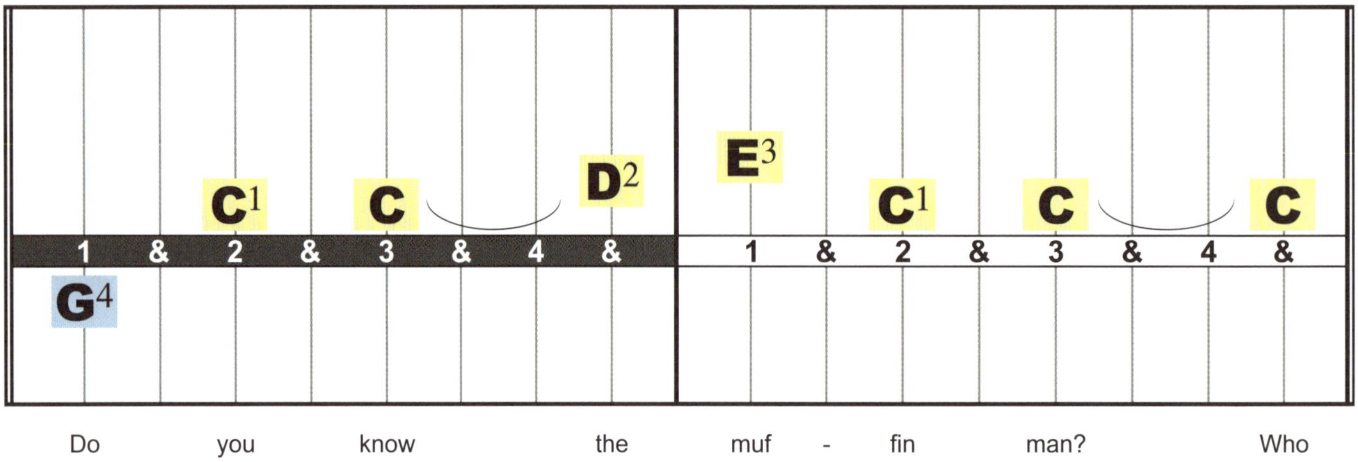

D[2]		D						C[1]							
1	&	2	&	3	&	4	&	1	&	2	&	3	&	4	&
				G[4]		G									

lives on Muf - fin Lane.

Head, Shoulders, Knees, and Toes

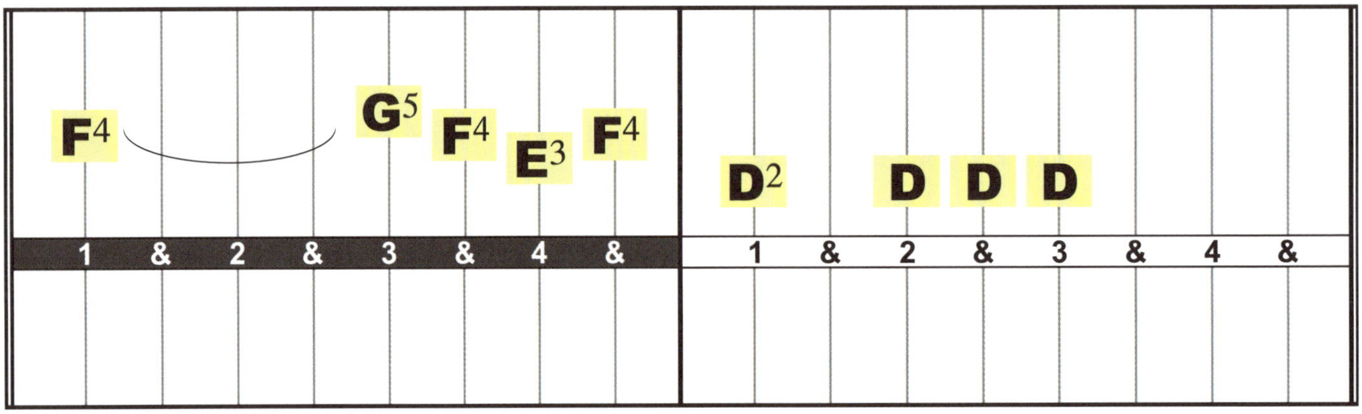

Head, shoul - ders, knees, and toes knees and toes

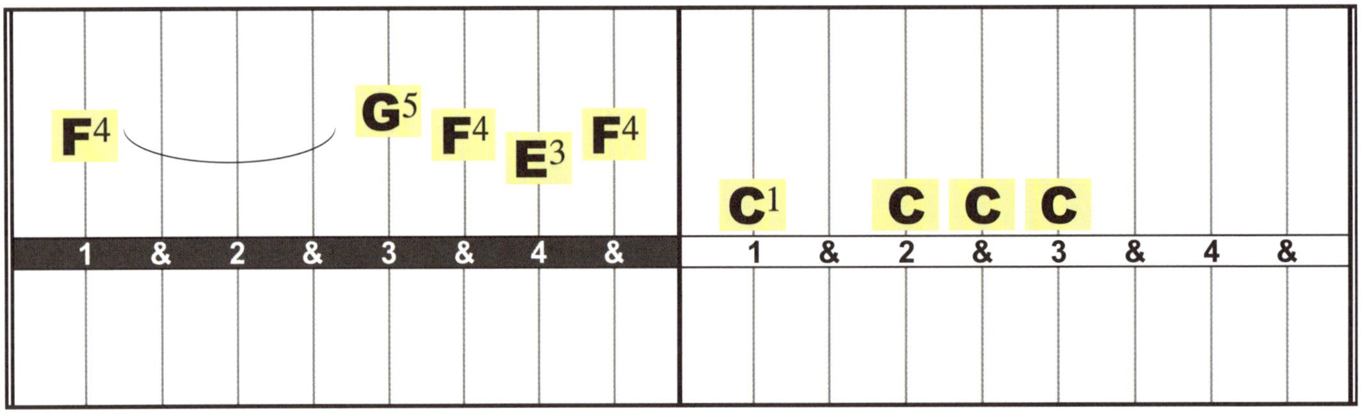

Head, shoul - ders, knees, and toes knees and toes

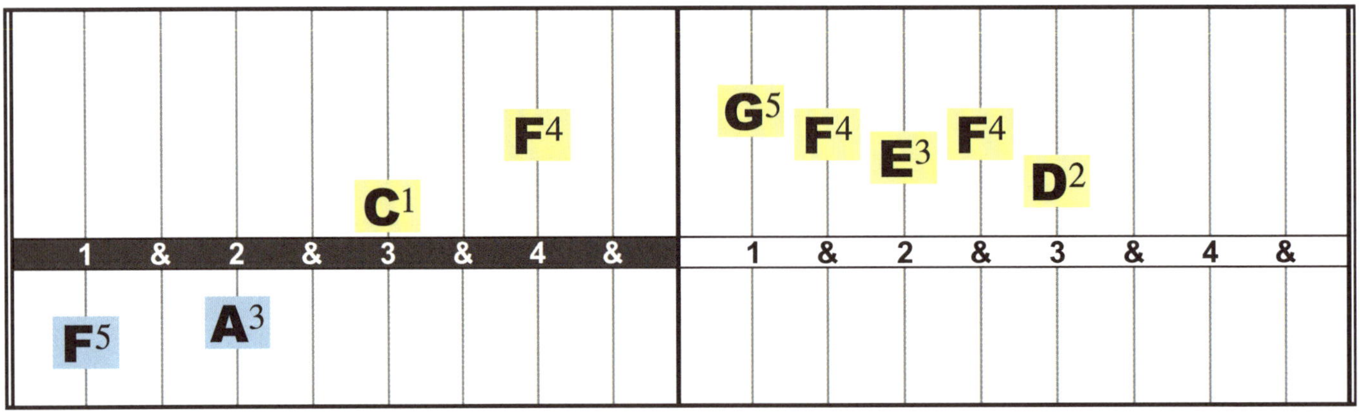

eyes and ears and mou - th an - d nose

1	&	2	&	3	&	4	&	1	&	2	&	3	&	4	&
E^3				E	C^1	D^2	E^3	F^4		F	F	F			
Head,				shoul -	ders,	knees,	and	toes		knees	and	toes			

The Baby Bumblebee

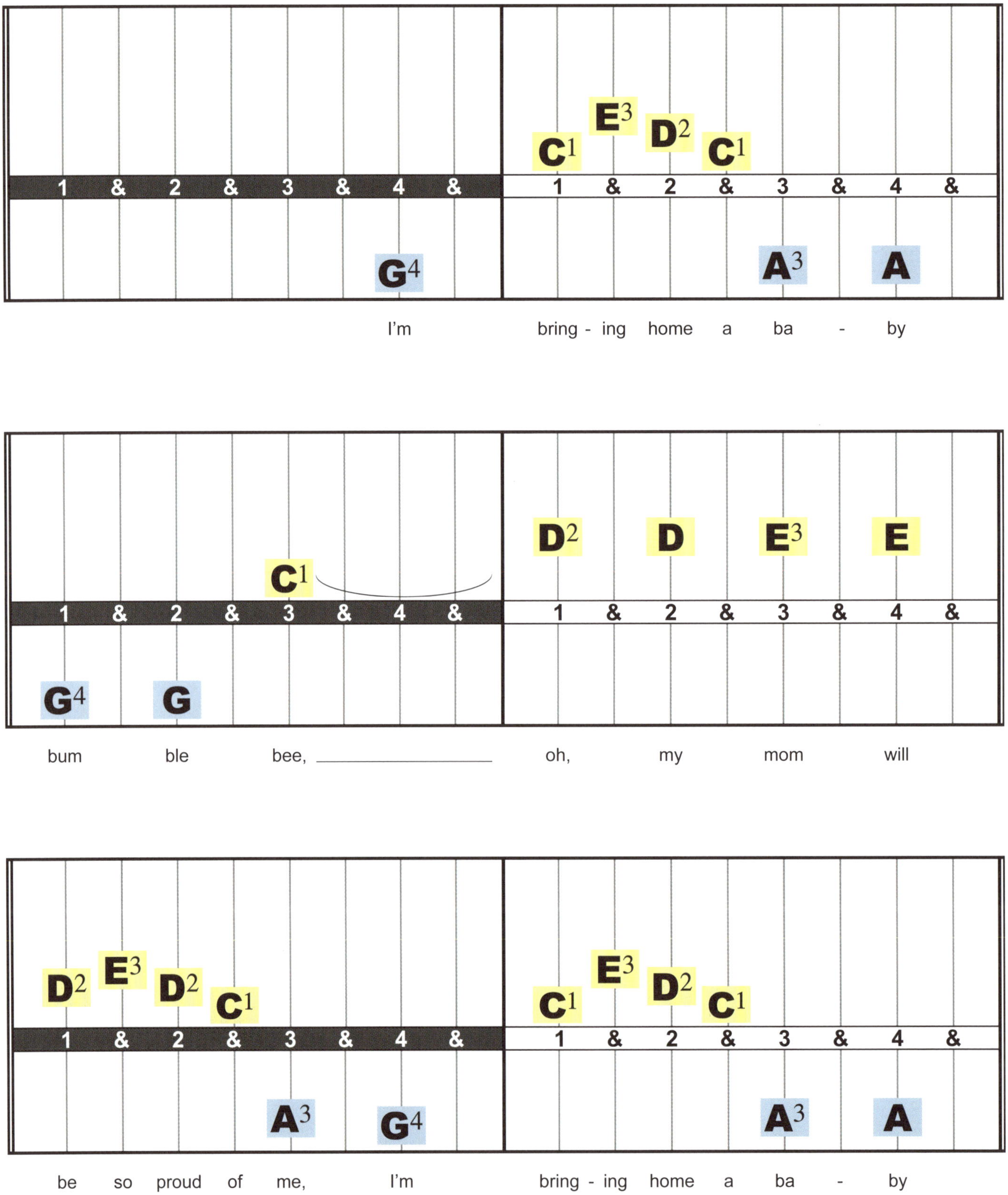

				C^1												
1	**&**	**2**	**&**	**3**	**&**	**4**	**&**	**1**	**&**	**2**	**&**	**3**	**&**	**4**	**&**
G^4		G						C^1	B^2	C^1	G^4	A^3	C^1	B^2	A^3
bum	-	ble		bee											

1	**&**	**2**	**&**	**3**	**&**	**4**	**&**
G^4		B^2		C^1			
Ow! it		stung		me!			

Hokey Pokey

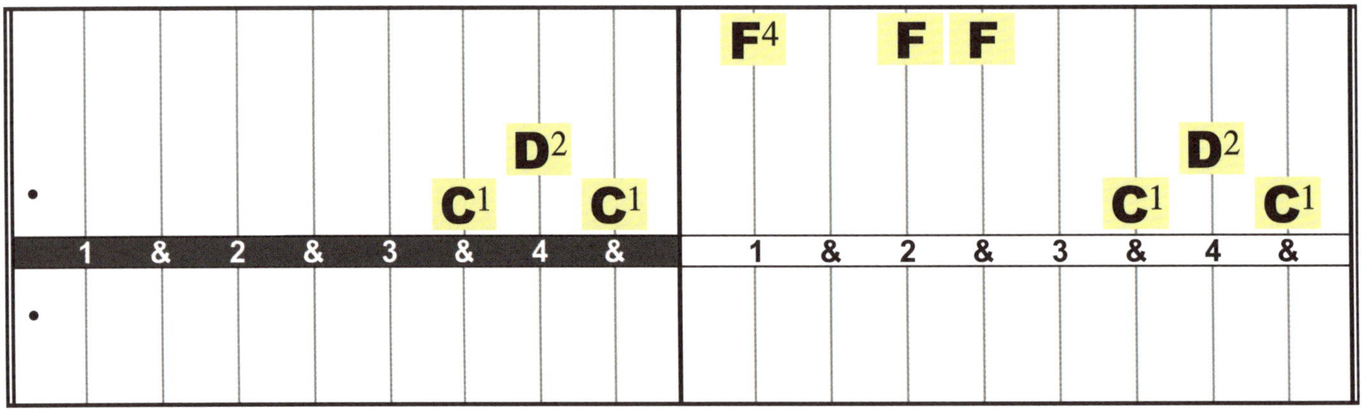

1. You put your right foot in. You take your
2. You put your left foot in. You take your

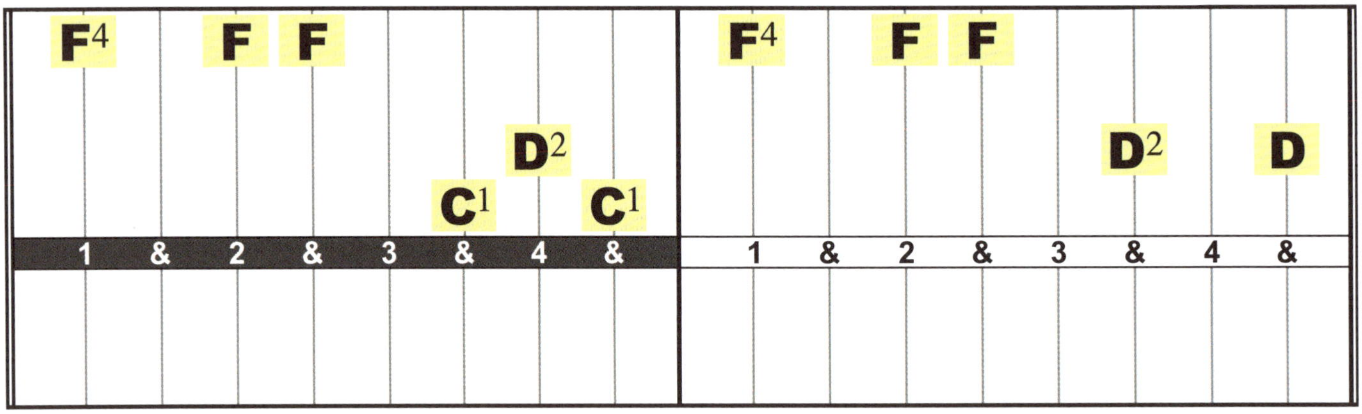

right foot out. You put your right foot in, and you
left foot out. You put your left foot in, and you

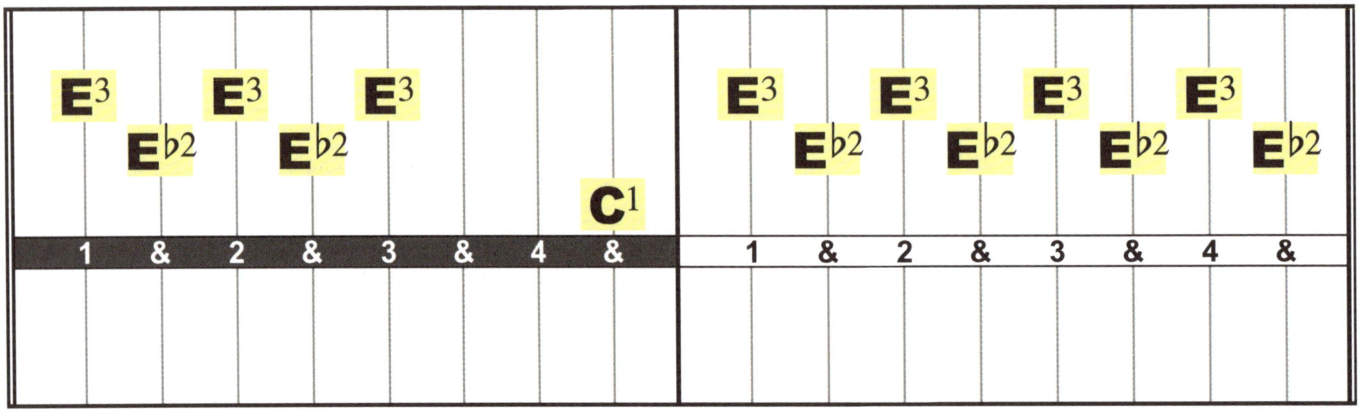

Shake it all a - bout. You do the Ho - key Po - key and you
Shake it all a - bout. You do the Ho - key Po - key and you

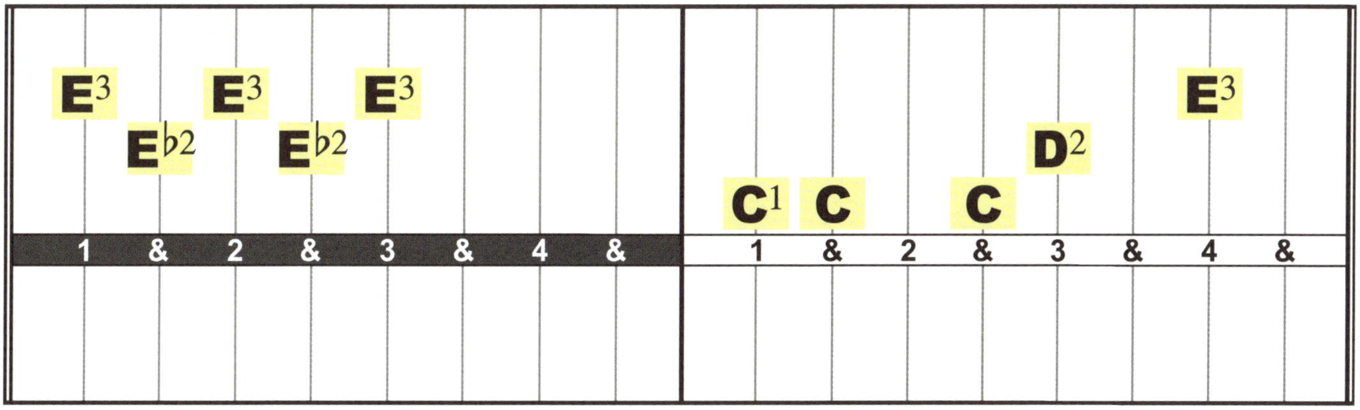

shake it all a - bout. That's what it's all a ———
shake it all a - bout. That's what it's all a ———

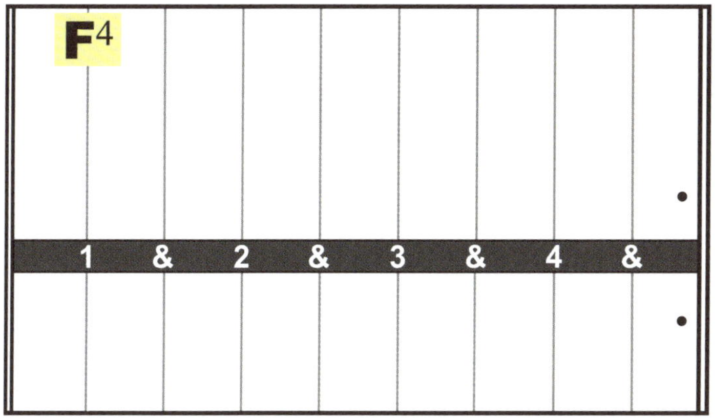

bout.
bout.

1 & 2 & 3 & 4 & 1 & 2 & 3 & 4 &

1 & 2 & 3 & 4 & 1 & 2 & 3 & 4 &

1 & 2 & 3 & 4 & 1 & 2 & 3 & 4 &

1 & 2 & 3 & 4 & 1 & 2 & 3 & 4 &

1 & 2 & 3 & 4 & 1 & 2 & 3 & 4 &

1 & 2 & 3 & 4 & 1 & 2 & 3 & 4 &

1 & 2 & 3 & 4 & 1 & 2 & 3 & 4 &

1 & 2 & 3 & 4 & 1 & 2 & 3 & 4 &

1 & 2 & 3 & 4 & 1 & 2 & 3 & 4 &

1	&	2	&	3	&	4	&	1	&	2	&	3	&	4	&

1	&	2	&	3	&	4	&	1	&	2	&	3	&	4	&

1	&	2	&	3	&	4	&	1	&	2	&	3	&	4	&

KEYTAB Note Strip Instructions

The KEYTAB Note Strip fits behind the keys of any piano or keyboard. Cut out the sections below to get started. Scan the QR code or watch the video at this link:

youtube.com/shorts/m5Tje4hYYvQ

To get instructions on how to install the KEYTAB Note Strip on your piano. You can purchase an official patented two-sided KEYTAB Note Strip at **KeyTabMusic.com**.

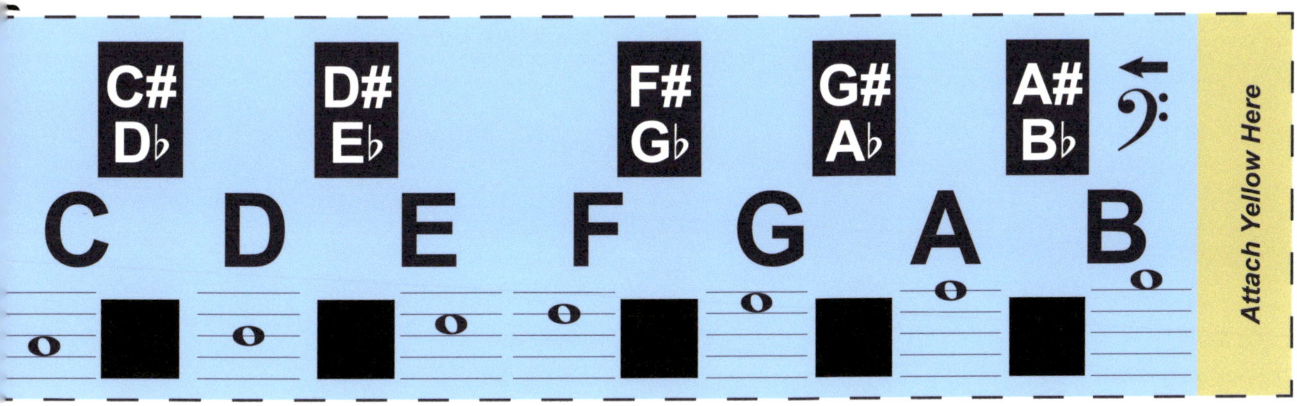
C# D♭
D# E♭
F# G♭
G# A♭
A# B♭
C D E F G A B
Attach Yellow Here

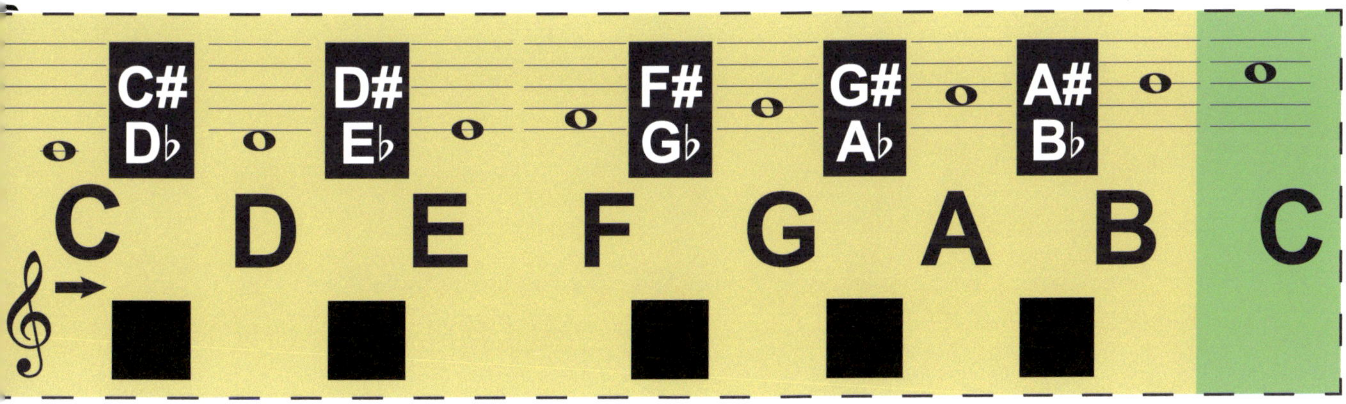
C# D♭
D# E♭
F# G♭
G# A♭
A# B♭
C D E F G A B C